This book is dedicated to
the thousands of youth who have made India
a global BPO superpower and revolutionized the lives
of millions around them.

BUSINESS PROCESS OUTSOURCING

Oh! BPO—
Structure and Chaos, Fun and Agony

V. Anandkumar (VAK)
Subhasish Biswas

Response
Business books from SAGE
Los Angeles ■ London ■ New Delhi ■ Singapore
www.sagepublications.com

First published in 2008 by

Response Books
Business books from SAGE
B1/I-1 Mohan Cooperative Industrial Area
Mathura Road, New Delhi 110 044, India

SAGE Publications Inc
2455 Teller Road
Thousand Oaks, California 91320, USA

SAGE Publications Ltd
1 Oliver's Yard, 55 City Road
London EC1Y 1SP, United Kingdom

SAGE Publications Asia-Pacific Pte Ltd
33 Pekin Street
#02-01 Far East Square
Singapore 048763

Published by Vivek Mehra for Response Books, typeset in 10/12pt Aldin401BT and printed at Chaman Enterprises, New Delhi.

Library of Congress Cataloging-in-Publication Data

Anandkumar, V.
    Business process outsourcing: oh! BPO—structure and chaos, fun and agony/
V. Anandkumar, Subhasish Biswas.
        p. cm.
    1. Offshore outsourcing—India. 2. Data processing service centres—India.
3. Computer service industry—India. I. Biswas, Subhasish. II. Title.

| HD2365.K875 | 658.4'0580954—dc22 | 2008 | 2008019789 |

ISBN: 978-81-7829-878-8 (PB)

The SAGE Team: Sugata Ghosh, Abantika Banerjee, Rajib Chatterjee and Trinankur Banerjee

Contents

Contents

List of Tables

List of Figures

List of Abbreviations

ACS	Affiliated Computer Services
AHT	average handling time
AOL	America Online
BA	British Airways
BOSS	burn out stress syndrome
BOT	build operate transfer
BSNL	Bharat Sanchar Nigam Limited
BU	business unit
CAGR	compound annual growth rate
CDO	chief development officer
CEO	chief executive officer
CFO	chief finance officer
CIO	chief information officer
CLO	chief learning officer
COO	chief operating officer
COPC	Customer Operations Performance Centre
CRM	customer relationship management
CSAT	customer satisfaction
CSPs	customer service providers
CTC	cost to company
CTO	chief training officer
DNC	do not call
EBIDTA	earnings before interest, depreciation, taxes, and amortization
EPS	earning per share
ERP	enterprise resource planning

FAQs	frequently asked questions
F&A	finance and accounting
FDI	foreign direct investment
GE	General Electric
GECIS	General Electric Capital International Services
GMs	general managers
HCL	Hindustan Computers Limited
HP	Hewlett-Packard
IIT	Indian Institute of Technology
IJP	internal job posting
IPO	initial public offer
IT	information technology
ITES	information technology enabled services
KPO	knowledge processes outsourcing
LIC	Life Insurance Corporation
M&As	mergers and acquisitions
MIS	management information system
MNC	multinational corporation
MTNL	Mahanagar Telephone Nigam Limited
NASSCOM	National Association of Software and Services Companies
NCR	National Capital Region
OJT	on the job training
PAN	permanent account number
PBIT	profit before income tax
PF	provident fund
QBR	quarter business review
RBI	Reserve Bank of India
RFPs	request for proposals
RPH	rate per hour
RPO	recruitment process outsourcing
R&R	rewards and recognition
SBU	strategic business unit

SEZs	special economic zones
SLA	service level agreement
SPOC	single point of contact
TCS	Tata Consultancy Service
TL	team leader
T&M	time and material
VC	venture capital
WFM	workforce management
YoY	year on year

Foreword

Business Process Outsourcing is a unique book. It is simple, straightforward, and well laid out. Most importantly, it is one book that gets to the core of the issues and concerns regarding the BPO industry. It does not beat around the bush; it calls a spade a spade.

It is an excellent guide to anyone who wants to get inducted into the Indian BPO industry. Not only does it cover all the aspects of the industry, but also provokes thought into changes that are needed to sustain growth over the years.

Business Process Outsourcing would appeal to a manager in the BPO industry, an 18-year-old looking for her first job, and also to her family and friends. It provides valuable information to people planning to shift careers from other industries to the world of BPO, and orients customers in understanding the nuances of the Indian BPO business. It can help entrepreneurs identify the trends and the opportunities in the industry and will certainly make many chief executive officers of the BPO industry ponder on the direction they have taken and contemplate on the road ahead.

Lastly, it will help the media to understand the positives of the industry and the role that this industry has played in shaping the careers of over 600,000 young people in India. This will hopefully make them proactive in supporting the industry by presenting a realistic picture. Constructive and positive communication from the press will go a long way in sustaining and increasing the confidence of the industry—something that is very critical as the industry starts expanding into smaller towns.

It is in this context that I applaud the kind of efforts put in by VAK (V. Anandkumar) and Subhasish in presenting a candid and compelling picture of the BPO industry in India, and I am sure this book will play a role in changing the direction of the BPO industry in India in the years to come!

Madan Padaki
Co-founder and CEO
MeritTrac Services

Preface

Our journey in the fast growing BPO industry over the last few years has been a roller-coaster ride. The beauty of this industry is that it gets you so involved that at times you feel you have spent a lifetime here. Every day has its own share of excitement and challenges. We have been through all the upheavals, walked the path of structure and chaos, and tasted its fun and agony.

During this time, we have interacted with thousands of 'BPOites' from all over the country, candidates wanting to join the industry, a wide array of people in the age group of 18–55 years, people supporting the industry from outside, the press, our customers, and thought leaders. And these were the people who helped us with their views and ideas in putting this book together.

BPO today is front-page news—pick any magazine, newspaper or switch on a news channel and you will find one view or another about the BPO industry. However, not all of them are always positive, or depict the true picture of the industry.

The industry is unique and attracts people from a wide cross section. It has acted as an inclusive engine of growth expanding beyond metros to smaller towns. People joining the industry come from a wide variety of backgrounds. There are many who have joined from the hospitality, transportation, airlines, and manufacturing industries, from sales, banking, retail, the armed forces, and so on.

We realized that most people joining and working in the industry had limited knowledge about the full world of a BPO. Their perspective was sketchy, based on hearsay, and what they had read in magazines and newspapers.

The most important aspect of BPOs is that every year about 150,000 fresh graduates and undergraduates join the industry, earning their first pay cheque from the BPO industry.

This book attempts to present the world of BPO in a simple manner; it can be read and understood in 4–5 hours; it contains information that is useful and thought provoking. We are hopeful that we will be able to fill a void that exists today.

We realized that the opportunities and challenges of the nascent BPO business were unique and were keen to look at this in-depth. So, not only have we compiled and illustrated the issues that affect the industry, but have also provided solutions to address them.

We started this book with a view to creating a guide for every person who wanted to join the industry. The book looks at the structure and issues in a BPO from the perspective of the employee, employer, and the customer. There are also some misconceptions and myths associated with the industry. It was important to provide comprehensive information in order to dispel these misperceptions.

We expect this book to be of great use to every new recruit. It seeks to provide a complete and easy comprehension of the industry and help her get a better perspective. And this would be the first step towards right-selling a career in the BPO industry.

It is an attempt to present the ground reality—a guide for anyone wanting to get initiated into the BPO world. It is a good simple read for every parent who wants to see their children work in a BPO.

We met many customers who were contemplating setting up their own BPO centres or entering into a partnership for outsourcing work to India. And like most others, they too had scarce and patchy information about the reality of the Indian BPO industry. They wished for exhaustive information—a bible on the Indian BPO industry—and we wanted to ensure that we could provide them the information that they were looking for, so that they could take a conscious and well-informed decision. Prospective customers wanting to outsource work to India will find this book insightful.

This volume will help people working in the BPO industry to understand how to improvise on the functioning of their organizations. It is a guide that will help educate the press about the positives and challenges of the industry.

We looked at the positives and the opportunities thrown up by the industry. We wanted the industry to be proud of its achievements and be conscious of its weaknesses. *This book is an attempt to create Brand BPO.*

Business Process Outsourcing presents a balanced view of the industry from the perspective of an insider. It explains structured chaos.

Most importantly, we wanted industry leaders and companies to stop and think about the road ahead. The game has just begun. There is a need to step back and reflect on the changes that need to be made to make the business healthy and robust. The core message being—think long term versus short term, be profitable, beat global standards, but do not let avarice get the better of you, invest for the future, invest in human capital and technology.

The industry has a social responsibility in ensuring that the youth of today lead productive and fruitful lives 15 years from today. It is time we mix the rational rush for growth and profit with an emotional thought about the workforce and their future.

Starting with a detailed industry overview, we look at the issues in managing a BPO and the changes in the last seven years. We then move on to the employee perspective where we elaborate on the real life of a young BPO employee. In the chapter on 'The Future of BPOs' (Chapter 5), we look at the possible upsides and downsides of the industry. And finally, the last chapter on 'Points to Ponder' (Chapter 6) throws up debates on fundamental issues in running a business and their correlation with BPOs.

We have included interesting data and pointers that can help readers define their strategy, and have enumerated varied examples from different industries, which we have bridged with the BPO industry. This volume is not a moral science text on 'do's' and 'don'ts', but a book with a good mix of the rational and the emotional. With this caveat, read on.

Acknowledgements

The spark for writing this book came to us during an internal meeting of our team when we were debating means and methods of hiring the right talent by right-selling jobs at Wipro BPO. We would like to thank our colleagues for encouraging and helping us get started.

Our discussions with industry veterans, Madan Padaki, Piyush Mehta, Sandeep Dhar, Nagraj Shanmugam, Milind Godbole, Sudip Nandi, Alok Jain, Sai Babu, Ravi Venkatesh, Saju Joseph, and Aashu Kalappa helped us expand our thought process and gain keen insights into the working of BPOs across the country. Many thanks also to Praveen Kamath.

Shombit Sengupta provided us with unique perspectives, which only he can. Our good friend Ashok Agrawal shared with us his simple ideas on how to retain and motivate teams.

Dr Jagdish Sheth gave us very interesting insights about the BPO industry in the United States (US) and steps that we need to take to make the workforce stable. We got a deep insight into the BPO business in the Philippines from Carol.

We have referred to Gartner reports, National Association of Software and Services Companies (NASSCOM) reports, and McKinsey reports for data points. We have also found useful information from the *Global Call Centre Report*. The *CLSA Report* (www.clsa.com) on information technology (IT) BPO helped us understand the impact of the industry on the surrounding economy.

A special thanks to our friend and writer Namita Gupta, who helped us in editing and styling the book.

Finally, we would like to thank our families for their encouragement and support.

CHAPTER 1

The BPO Industry

Life in India has changed, thanks to the growth in the domain of information technology (IT) and business process outsourcing (BPO). It has transformed an entire generation.

The history of outsourcing dates back to mythological times. It is said that when Sage Ved Vyasa wanted to write the epic Mahabharata, he looked around for someone who would write down the words even as he recited them. He approached Lord Ganesha and asked him if he would do so. Lord Ganesha readily agreed to do so. We call this data entry today.

Ganesha had one criterion before accepting the job—the learned Ved Vyasa could not take a break while reciting the epic. If he stopped at any time, Ganesha would stop writing and the epic would stay incomplete.

Ved Vyasa agreed with this condition, 'I agree, but you must also agree to fully comprehend the meaning of the poems as you write and not just blindly write them as I recite them.'

These were the first set of service level agreements (SLAs) that were decided between the outsourcing partners.

What started in ages long ago has today become a thriving industry that provides a livelihood to millions. The work done by a BPO is nothing novel. The work done by a ticketing agent, a scribe in a court, a receptionist, an accountant in an office, a teller in a bank—is exactly the kind of work that is done by a BPO company. The only change is that the work has now been aggregated. As organizations focus on their core competency, the peripheral work gets outsourced to companies that specialize in doing these activities by hiring and training people.

When the work gets aggregated at the global level, you realize that there are actually millions of jobs that can be aggregated and done in a manner that reduces costs and improves efficiency.

According to Pascal's Law, fluids find their uniform level. In the same way, BPO work from all corners of the globe finds its way to destinations that can deliver quality output at economical prices.

This trend has helped countries like India and the Philippines change the work environment of teeming millions by giving them gainful employment. It has helped the economy grow and set the foundation for rapid globalization.

The BPO revolution has been possible in India due to two important factors—the strong legacy of English language education left behind by the British, who ruled India for nearly 200 years, and the adoption of English as the national language by the Indian government in 1965.

The Constitution of India came into existence on 26 January 1950. Enshrined in the Constitution was the status of Hindi and English as the 'official languages' of the central government till 1965 (for a period of 15 years), after which Hindi was expected to take up the pre-eminent position as the sole 'national and official language' of India. However, among non-Hindi speakers, especially those in southern India, apprehension grew as this date approached. It became clear that the non-Hindi speaking population would be denied the much coveted government jobs and teaching opportunities as it was proposed that after 1965 all national examinations would be conducted in Hindi.

The pro-Hindi fanatics in the Jan Sangh prowled the streets of New Delhi, blackening out any signs in English. According to Annadurai, a powerful figure in south India, you could speak Tamil and English and still be a good Indian.

The anti-Hindi agitations also led to the demand for the creation of Dravidistan, a separate state for the speakers of the Dravidian languages (the languages spoken in south India). While some others considered it a result of the divide and rule principle of the British, a coterie of the Congress comprising such stalwarts as S. Nijalingappa (chief minister of Mysore), Kamaraj (Congress president), Sanjiva Reddy (union minister) and Atulya Ghosh (Bengal Congress president) realized the gravity of the situation and asked Prime Minister Shastri to revoke the policy of making Hindi the sole 'national language'.

Shastri, even though supportive of the pro-Hindi group, realized the seriousness of the issue and came up with a set of compromises that did not give Hindi any 'sole national language' status. Most importantly, English was not removed as the medium for competitive examinations like the All India Civil Services Examination. Also, transactions between the states and the centre were to be conducted in the official language of the state concerned together with an English translation. For example, communication from Tamil Nadu to the central government was to be in Tamil and English; communication from the centre to Tamil Nadu was to be in English and Hindi. Thus, the 1965 anti-Hindi agitation subsided.

This decision in 1965 was momentous. It ensured that Indians would have a good foundation in English. When we look back, both the IT and the BPO revolutions have been possible thanks to the proficiency of Indians in English. That is the edge we have over other countries, like China, today.

As we embark on this book let us take a quick look at how some lives have been transformed courtesy the BPO industry.

Sundar used to work as a delivery boy for a pizza chain. Family circumstances forced him to take up a job very early in life. One night, while delivering pizzas to a local BPO company, he interacted with the vice president (VP), human resources (HR), of the company while settling the bill. In the brief conversation that he had with Sundar, the VP felt that his communication skills were good and called him in for an interview the next day. Sundar was a graduate in arts and a confident person. He came out with flying colours at the interview and joined the BPO in 2001 at a starting salary of Rs 8,000. Over the years he spent long hours in his job, he learnt the tricks of the trade and excelled. He was a star performer who went up the rungs very rapidly. Today, Sundar is an associate vice president (AVP) and manages a large client relationship. He is based in the US and is a telecom domain specialist. Thanks to this job, he has got his sisters married and has recently booked a two-bedroom flat in Whitefield in Bangalore.

Prasenjit was the eldest son in a middle-class family of four. His father worked as an administrative assistant in a college. When Prasenjit was 19, his father had a heart attack and passed away. At the time, Prasenjit was in the second year at college. The family had limited savings. They were living in a house for which they had taken a Rs 400,000 loan. Realizing the challenge the family was facing, Prasenjit decided to take up a job. Talking to a few friends he realized that the quickest way to earn money was to join a BPO company. He applied to a few BPO companies and got selected to one of them.

Prasenjit used to work at night and study during the day. The first few years were tough and he barely managed to get a few winks. Determined to succeed he ploughed along. He managed to complete his degree and the company reimbursed his fees. He changed a few roles in the same company and became a well-accomplished 'BPOite'.

Today, five years later, Prasenjit is a senior manager in the company. He manages a team of 250 people. He earns Rs 800,000 per annum, his house loan is fully paid off, and he has just bought his first car. He is now getting married to a colleague from the same BPO. Life has almost taken a complete turn for him.

Sanjeev Bhatia hails from a business family. His father used to run a small photocopying shop at Connaught Place in New Delhi. During the riots of 1984, their shop was burnt to rubble and they were on the streets. Sanjeev took a loan of Rs 100,000 and started a small business. This business got impetus when he started working with the BPO units of General Electric (GE) and American Express (AMEX), becoming their logistics partner for stationery. His business grew rapidly thanks to the growth of these BPO companies in the 1990s. In 1999, when Raman Roy was starting Spectramind, he asked Sanjeev to be part of the core team. Sanjeev started as an executive assistant to Raman and grew rapidly within the organization to manage teams of over 2,000 people in the operations department. Today he is a VP at Wipro BPO and heads the international operations and customer advocacy departments.

Lakshmi Ranganathan is a post-graduate in mathematics. She is a housewife and a mother of two. Her husband works in a bank and draws a modest salary. Domestic responsibilities, including having to take care of her children and her in-laws, forced Lakshmi to stay at home and not take up a job. While surfing the web, Lakshmi found an option to provide tutorial help to high school students in the United States (US). She registered and very soon a girl from Ohio contacted her. Lakshmi today spends two hours on the computer with a headphone tutoring the girl in mathematics. She gets paid US$ 10 an hour. The money is transferred to her bank account in Chennai. The arrangement works well—Lakshmi stays at home and takes care of her domestic responsibilities and earns more money than her husband. This is a classic case of how the internet is helping in consumer process outsourcing (CPO).

These are some examples of how BPOs have helped change the lives of people in India. If not for BPOs, Sundar, Sanjeev, Prasenjit and many others like them would have taken a trajectory very different from where they are today. And Lakshmi would have been in depression for having wasted her 18 years of education on changing diapers and cooking.

There are thousands of such examples across the world of BPOs. Each one is a touching tale of how this industry has helped and transformed the lives of simple people, how it has given them a launching pad to take off, and how these smart simple people have taken the opportunity and never looked back. It is an industry that has helped and given so much to the people who have joined it. It has no parallels, yet it is sad to see the way in which the BPO industry in India is looked upon.

Let us analyse and get a deeper insight into the real Indian BPO industry.

The Foundation Years: An Overview

Like a tsunami, every revolution starts slowly and then accelerates. BPO firms in India that started off in the early 1990s have seen a similar transformation and are today on the threshold of creating a revolution that touches not only the 600,000 people directly employed by them, but millions of others who are associated with them.

The industry has notched up revenues in excess of US$ 7 billion in 2007 and is all set to exceed US$ 10 billion in the next few years. In short, the BPO industry has achieved in less than a decade what the IT industry took over 20 years to achieve.

As the industry has grown from a zero base, it has absorbed people from different industries. Today, it stands out as a unique business that employs the largest variety of professionals—graduates, undergraduates, chartered accountants (CAs), people with bachelors of commerce (B.Com) degrees, engineers, people with masters of business administration (MBA) degrees, graphic designers, animation experts, investment bankers, data entry operators, presentation specialists, lawyers, paralegal assistants, equity research specialists, analysts, doctors, etc. You will find all these and more in a BPO company.

Give a thought to what would have happened to all the young boys and girls in the country if the BPO juggernaut had not arrived. Many of the people working in BPOs today have only completed their high school examinations and are not even graduates. Has anyone thought of the purchasing power of this group? The more they earn, the more is spent, helping the economy grow.

This is nothing short of a revolution—a wave that has swept across the country and impacted lives across metros and smaller towns, the tremors of which have been felt globally. And this wave can continue for the next decade. *Globally, there are over 30 million BPO jobs and till date less than 600,000 million have landed on the shores of India.*

BPO companies in India have been growing at a compound annual growth rate (CAGR) of over 40 per cent for the last seven years. Not only have they provided gainful employment to millions, they have also made millionaires of many young entrepreneurs who have set up businesses closely associated with the BPO industry like recruitment consultancies, travel agencies, cafeteria services, training centres, and other ancillary businesses that support this frenetic growth.

Most people co-relate BPO companies with call centres. The reality is that only 50 per cent of the Indian BPO industry comprises call centres. The rest are manned by highly skilled professionals, working real time on global problems for Fortune 500 companies.

The value proposition of a BPO company is simple—if you are committed and serious, if you are ready to learn and achieve, have a decent education, good interpersonal skills, and are ready to work 8–10 hours a day, you have an assured job offering a minimum salary in the range of Rs 8,000–15,000 (US$ 200–375) a month.

Over the years, BPO companies and employees have also had their share of unique challenges. While there has been speedy volume growth, it is questionable if there has been any value growth.

While thousands have been gainfully employed, it is strongly debated if the BPO industry in India is a finishing school or the first step to a well-rounded career. Is it an easy entry-level job with a good starting salary and perks, or is it just a stepping stone? Are companies doing enough to create a long-term career for a fresher joining the BPO industry? Do we need engineers and highly qualified graduates working as customer support executives? Are we building a generation of youth who may not be able to scale their career beyond 10 years? What would be the impact of a slowdown in the industry on these people?

These are questions that this young industry needs to answer to ensure that growth continues on a solid foundation. These are some debatable topics and we need to think of lucid answers for them; answers which will determine the next phase of growth for the industry.

There has also been some negative publicity about BPO and call centres. Many parents are apprehensive about sending their daughters to work in night shifts. There is a sense of suspicion about anything associated with BPOs. The press has not played a very productive role in positioning this nascent industry in the correct manner.

While apprehensions about the BPO industry have reduced significantly from their early days, there are still some issues of concern. The rape and murder of Pratibha Murthy and Tanya Banerjee of Bangalore and Jyoti Choudhry of Pune, all employees of BPO firms, have added to this concern and raised valid questions about security and the processes in place. Is the industry investing in the necessary technology and systems to make the processes foolproof or are we praying that all goes well day after day in this world of structured chaos? Have we been able to think through all the loopholes and plug them effectively?

The reality of the BPO industry is often blurred and the glamour associated with its early days seems to be fading. The achievements and challenges of this industry are unique. Its positives can definitely outdo its challenges. BPO firms and individuals associated with them need to apply serious thought towards strengthening the foundation of the industry and making it more robust.

Even chief executive officers (CEOs) and chief operating officers (COOs) seem to be helpless in solving the problems that plague the industry, with attrition being the most important problem.

What is the real cause of attrition? Are genuine efforts being made to tackle this problem or are we getting bogged down by having to analyse too many data points? Is there paralysis from analysis?

The reason for attrition is addressed in depth and discussed at length later.

Let Us Get to Know What BPO is

BPO stands for business process outsourcing. Let us understand what this means:

1. You go to a bank and open a new account. The form gets updated by *someone* in the system and you soon get a mail with your new account number and password.

2. After you travel and come back to office you submit your bills, *someone* checks it and credits the amount to your bank account.

3. You buy a mobile phone and *someone* in the service provider's back office needs to set you up on the network and provision you with the right set of services.

4. A research professor wants to get details on a certain area and does not have time to surf through a detailed website. He seeks the help of *someone* like a research assistant.

5. An insurance company wants to identify the highest liability age group for a certain product. They have the data, but want *someone* to analyse it.

6. Your personal computer (PC) crashes and you need to get it fixed in time for an urgent presentation. You call up the toll-free number of your PC's manufacturer and *someone* helps you troubleshoot and solve the problem.

7. You need to book a ticket and call the leading airline company. *Someone* helps you with the best rates, books your ticket, charges your credit card, and sends you confirmation by email.

8. There is an accident (in the US) and a call is placed to 911. *Someone* takes the call and sets in motion a series of actions aimed at solving the injured person's problem at the earliest.

These are all examples of business processes that happen in everyday life across industries worldwide. Most people working in companies across the globe would be doing these jobs on a day-to-day basis. The work done by that *someone* is what we are referring to as potentially 'outsourceable' work.

Given the lack of resources and the high cost of labour in developed countries, much of this work is getting outsourced to developing low-cost locations like India, the Philippines, east Europe, China, etc., thanks to an excellent low-cost telecom network.

The cost to company (CTC) of an entry-level accountant in the US may be upwards of US$ 36,000 per year. The same job can be done in India by a commerce graduate whose CTC would be less than US$ 5,000 a year. Multiply this saving over millions of jobs the world over and it is easy to understand why the outsourcing boom is growing by leaps and bounds.

Savings from labour arbitrage is a key benefit of the global outsourcing business. Developed economies have higher minimum wages and taxes. The cost of living is extremely high compared to developing countries. The growth of China and Taiwan in manufacturing, India and east Europe in IT, and India and the Philippines in call centres and BPO firms are classic examples of large corporations using global cost economics to their advantage.

However, in BPO, the scope for benefit goes far beyond labour arbitrage. It is often said that the 'O' in BPO stands for optimization. This can be achieved by analysing the work to be outsourced and by adding value to the process so that the client gets maximum benefit. Some BPO practitioners feel that in the years to come, the benefits from optimization will far exceed the gains from labour arbitrage.

In principle, BPO arrangements allow a company to focus on its strategic core activities and cut costs on other activities by outsourcing them without compromising on service levels and customer satisfaction. A well-run outsourcing agreement is a win–win relationship for both partners.

The activities that are usually outsourced are those that are repetitive in nature and are done frequently. If creating the records for a new subscriber takes 15 minutes and one can devise a new process, which does it in 12 minutes, you have knocked away 3 minutes from millions of such processes that happen every year. The savings thus accrued are colossal.

The combined effect of labour arbitrage and the benefits of optimization is what has made the BPO industry grow rapidly.

While labour arbitrage is a country value proposition, benefits from optimization are what industry leaders can provide their customers. From that perspective, the BPO industry does have a close linkage to the consulting business.

As the markets get crowded and more players join the BPO bandwagon, the leaders will establish themselves as not just cost leaders through scale, but also provide value in other areas.

While the trigger starts with cost saving through labour arbitrage, from a long-term sustainable view, leading BPO practitioners need to differentiate themselves by delivering value through more efficient processes.

The world of business transformation outsourcing may be split under three broad heads:

1. Process outsourcing—BPO.
2. IT outsourcing—application, maintenance, and development.
3. Infrastructure outsourcing.

As the industry matures, customers will derive higher benefits in outsourcing the entire pie rather than small discrete processes. The process of evaluating a partner, signing SLAs and contracts, and putting a project into action is a time-consuming one. There are close linkages between the three areas of work discussed earlier, which can be handled more efficiently to reduce costs and use the labour pool optimally.

The next phase of outsourcing will see more integrated business transformation deals, which are multi-billion dollar contracts spread over 5–10 years.

Integrated IT-BPO organizations are better suited to win these contracts. This is in line with what we see in India. Most companies that started their operations with call centres and scaled their business with them, are increasingly looking at growth from knowledge process outsourcing (KPO) and the non-voice side of business. The scope for intelligent optimization here is immense. India's large educated population is well suited to meet these requirements.

Legal process outsourcing, medical transcription, remote diagnostics, sales order processing, procurement, claims processing, finance and accounts services, insurance claims processing, mortgage processing, securities underwriting, equity research, secretarial services, language translation, etc.—the list can go on in terms of the work that can get outsourced.

The biggest difference between KPO/transaction processing and the call centre business is a less stringent demand on voice communication. Indians by nature are introverts and a very small percentage of the population can communicate in a neutral accent. Expecting an Indian to talk like an American is the same as expecting an American to talk like a Tamil-speaking person. The beauty is that hundreds of thousands of Indians do it, while even a handful of Americans may not cross the bar.

In emerging countries like India and the Philippines, the word BPO is loosely used for any non-IT outsourcing work. Globally, contact centres or call centres as a business are distinctly separate from BPO. Given the dominance of India in the IT market, another term used to describe BPO/contact centre work is ITES (IT enabled services). Work done by voice-centric 'BPO' companies would normally be in the customer relationship management (CRM) space.

Evolution and Growth of the Indian BPO Industry

The origin of the BPO industry in India goes back to the mid-1980s. Several European airlines started using New Delhi as a base for their back office operations, British Airways (BA) being one of them. The BA captive was finally spun off as a separate organization called WNS, which is today one of the largest third-party BPO player in the banking, finance, security and insurance (BFSI) and travel sectors.

In the second half of the 1980s, AMEX consolidated its Japan-Asia Pacific (JAPAC) back office operations in New Delhi. This centre was headed by Raman Roy and several leading names of the BPO industry have been associated with it at some point in their careers.

GE and the vision of Jack Welsh has been one of the key drivers of the global outsourcing industry. Old timers in GE recount that Jack had a 70–70–70 vision. Seventy per cent of all IT/ BPO work in GE had to be outsourced. Of this 70 per cent had to be outsourced to developing countries and 70 per cent of this had to be outsourced to India. This philosophy has been followed in spirit and in action. GE's success has led to other companies emulating it.

In the 1990s, GE set up its back office operations in Gurgaon. Pramod Bhasin, the head of GE, hired Raman Roy and several of his management team from AMEX to start General Electric Capital International Service (GECIS). Raman Roy for the first time tried out voice operations from India. Around the same time, Citibank also started its back office operations and call centre at Chennai.

The results were promising and made GE ramp up their India presence and open offices at other locations. In 2004, GECIS was spun off by GE as a separate legal entity called Genpact. In August 2007, Genpact mopped up US$ 494.1 million through an initial public offer (IPO) of 35.2 million shares.

In 2000, armed with venture capital (VC) funding, Raman Roy started his own company called Spectramind. Having sold Spectramind to Wipro, Roy now runs a company called Quattro.

When Raman Roy and his team started Spectramind in 2000, the plan was to start a back office shop. However, the initial clients from whom they got business were companies like Dell and America Online (AOL), who wanted to outsource their technical helpdesk business. Since then the industry has not looked back.

At around the same time, an organization called EXL started in Noida, Efunds started its operations in Mumbai and Gurgaon, Daksh started its operations in Gurgaon, and 24x7 Customer and Customer Asset started their operations in Bangalore. While Daksh was acquired by IBM and Customer Asset by First Source, EXL, Efunds, and 24x7 continued to be successful players.

Many start-ups founded at that time built large capacity. Setting up a BPO is expensive and can cost up to US$ 7,000 per seat. Setting up a 1,000-seater BPO firm would cost in excess of US$ 7 million. Having created capacity, companies were hoping that the dot-com boom would translate into large customer service business through email and chat. Unfortunately, the dot-com business crashed in 2001. Start-ups had to do a quick course correction to ensure that the capacity they had built was utilized. The call centre business was a low-hanging fruit and they capitalized on that.

Industry Segregation

Players in the BPO industry may be segregated under four broad areas as indicated in Figure 1.1. The quality of work, rates, and challenges start getting more complex as we move up the chain. At this juncture, the Indian industry has scaled the levels of being a bulk task provider, process expert, and service line expert. A strong talent pool and the focus on quality and compliance have helped the industry scale and grow business across these three levels rapidly. The scope for continuous growth in this area is immense.

Figure 1.1: Industry Segregation

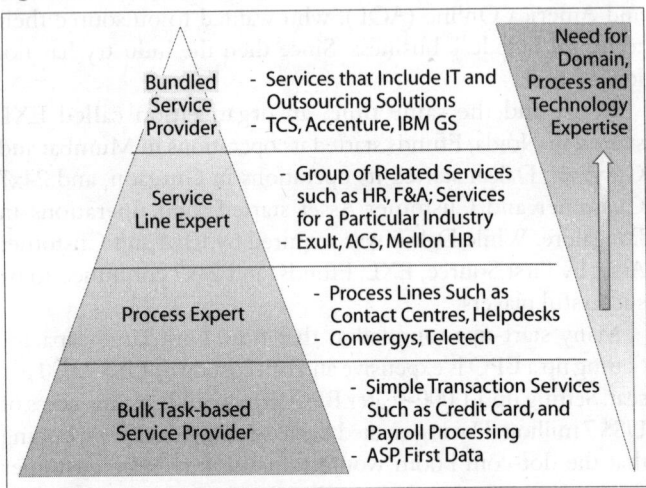

Source: Research conducted by the authors.

The big daddies of the business are keenly looking at the top tier of the business. That is an area where the global players like IBM, Accenture, and Capgemini have consolidated their place. Their consulting background has helped them win large turnkey contracts spread over extended durations. The jargon used for such deals is 'total outsourcing' and every year we see multi-billion dollar total outsourcing deals being awarded.

Getting back to basics, let us simplify the matter and say that the BPO industry can be broadly segregated into voice and non-voice processes. The non-voice component is also called transaction processing (TP). The key differences between the voice and non-voice components of the BPO industry are given in Table 1.1.

There is a world of difference between the two sets of businesses. The non-voice business has a closer relationship with the IT business. It is easier to get started and to scale up.

Table 1.1: Comparison between Voice and Non-Voice Processes

Voice	Non-Voice
Real time.	Real time and batch.
It is difficult to provide multi-country support because of language challenges.	Easier to provide multi-country support.
Customer identifies you with the brand. For example, a Dell computer user calling a call centre thinks he is talking to a representative from Dell.	Since it is not interactive, there is no direct correlation with a brand.
The focus of training is first on communication, accent, etc., before moving on to processes.	The focus is on processes.
Need for specialization in domain is limited.	Requires specialization and can evolve into a professional career track.
Errors, if any, have limited liability.	Errors/delays, if any, can have high liability. For example, change in interest rate can wipe away huge amounts of money if the work is not completed as scheduled.
Requires large investment in technology, links, etc.	Requires smaller investment.

Both, however, call for high levels of risk management and require high levels of adherence to compliance norms. The centres being set up for these businesses have to ensure foolproof safeguards against any malpractices. Data security and the use of technology are the keys to success in this industry. The perceived notion is that India scores over countries like China on these counts.

The client could also demand a dedicated floor space for specific critical processes, which could be accessible to the staff working for it. As part of the data protection drive, employees could be asked to sign a non-disclosure agreement and abide by it. As a security measure, BPO companies have embarked on policies that restrict employees from taking laptops, mobile phones, and cameras to the operation floors. The data scribbled by an employee while working on the floor needs to be shred before the employee leaves the operation floor. Data accessibility could be restricted as per the level of authority as prescribed by the authorization matrix in the procedure manual. Periodic audits will help in plugging the loopholes. The audits could be internal as well as client-mandated external audits.

The voice business may broadly be segregated under the following two categories:

1. Inbound.
2. Outbound.

During an inbound call, a customer calls a dedicated number or toll-free number in order to get information or help for resolving a problem. Examples of this would be:

1. A frequent flier calling an airline to check on his mileage points or to book a ticket.
2. A consumer calling a company to sort out a problem with a faulty device or to request the assistance of a service engineer.
3. A credit card user calling his bank to inquire about his transactions, check for any incorrect transactions, or to reset his password.
4. A consumer calling a trading house to buy or sell shares.

Inbound calls can be further classified as technical and non-technical calls. A technical call would be from the user of a product, for example, a PC or laptop, or router. A non-technical call would be from a person wanting to buy an airline ticket, a person seeking information on an enquiry service, a call to reset a password, or enquire about one's credit card balance. Technical calls tend to be longer, in some cases lasting 18–20 minutes. Non-technical calls tend to be less than 5 minutes in duration.

Outbound calls are normally collection, or sales calls. In a company specializing in outbound calls, there would be a battery of callers who keep calling existing and prospective customers. Samples of this would be:

1. Reminding a customer to pay his insurance premium.
2. Trying to sell credit cards/personal loans.
3. Follow up from a bank to remind a customer to pay credit card arrears.
4. Customer survey and feedback.

Outbound calling is like cold calling and can be very frustrating. Most outbound callers are measured on their effectiveness in selling and closing a deal, and in collection of dues. It would be normal to see an outbound caller making over 100 calls a day.

The entire load of balancing call volume is done through hi-tech gadgetry that distributes the load between multiple players across the globe. A caller calling in from the US could reach an agent in India, or the Philippines, or Mexico, or Canada, depending on the time and the nature of the call.

The World of Transaction Processing or Non-Voice BPO

Non-voice BPO has a more complex picture. The business here could be split under following areas:

1. Data entry, medical transcription, etc.
2. Rule-based processing like order processing, provisioning, finance and accounts, etc.
3. Domain-specific processing like investment banking, analytics, reporting and planning, research, audit, etc. This can be collectively termed as KPO.

KPO emerged as an acronym in the early 2000s as a marketing term to highlight the unique aspects of niche BPOs. These required workers to have deeper functional or domain expertise.

Unlike the voice BPO operations, non-voice operations are a complete paradigm shift and are closer in relationship to the IT business. This is the business on which people are betting on for future growth.

A transaction processing BPO firm is supposed to maintain agreed quality parameters as applicable to the process as the data/transaction worked upon could make or break a business. For example, processing a telegraphic transfer of a bank and sending money across the globe with the right exchange rate, currency, value date, and destination becomes very important. Any error would cause a delay. This delay would attract interest depending on the rates applicable as agreed by the bank with the customer. The customer sending/receiving money could also stand to lose significant amounts of money if there are any delays as the exchange rate fluctuates with time. Thus, the customer could incur secondary losses. Similarly, in an insurance-related BPO firm, if a claim is wrongly processed/reconciled, it may lead to serious litigation.

Although in a BPO firm there is no direct customer interface, it is very important to deliver quality services at least as per the agreed quality SLAs. Periodic quality audits would help to enhance the effectiveness and efficiency of the process.

Like call centres, non-voice BPO companies also base their business model on straight SLAs. At times, the SLAs for data processing could be much more stringent than calls as the time given to complete a work item is limited and errors could be disastrous as they could have serious financial and legal implications. The data handled is usually time critical and therefore time is money in a BPO. SLAs to complete a work item are usually measured in terms of rate per hour (RPH). This is usually fixed by the customer who is outsourcing the business. SLAs might depend upon time zones, currencies, and the nature of the data to be processed.

Companies are pegging their future on the growth of non-voice BPO. It is estimated that globally over 70 per cent of the BPO business and 25 million of the 30 million BPO jobs are accounted for by the transaction processing BPO firms.

A spate of new companies like MarketRx, μSigma, etc., have been set up in recent years that focus on very niche areas. Many of these companies have been acquired by larger BPO companies at astronomical valuations.

Figure 1.2: Areas of Work in BPO Companies and Comparative Rates (in US$/hour)

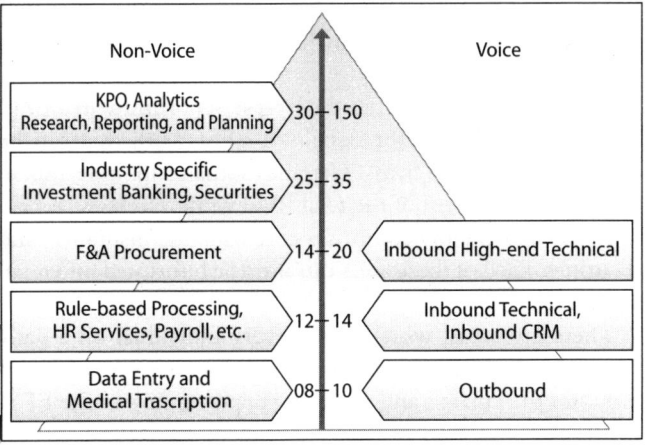

Source: Research conducted by authors.

Table 1.2: Examples of Industries Outsourcing Intellectually-Skilled Work

Example of Industries	Example of Activities
Health care	Clinical trials Clinical data management Statistical analysis
Legal	Research Litigation support Contract support Patent writing
Consumer products	Market research
Banking, finance, security, and insurance (BFSI)	Research Insurance underwriting and claims processing Mortgage processing Core banking
Engineering	Design Supply chain

The areas of work and the value chain for an integrated BPO organization in India would include the elements listed shown in Figure 1.2.

Finance-related work has the largest opportunity in a BPO firm. See Figure 1.3 for details of BFSI work that can be outsourced to BPO firms. Certain estimates indicate this to comprise 50 per cent of the total BPO work.

BFSI work mainly comprises core banking, insurance, and securities. Each of these areas can again be bifurcated into retail and business.

These are areas, which touch every individual on a daily basis and the transactional work here is colossal. Table 1.3 indicates the current and emerging opportunities in the BFSI BPO space.

Figure 1.3: Global BPO Work Outsourced

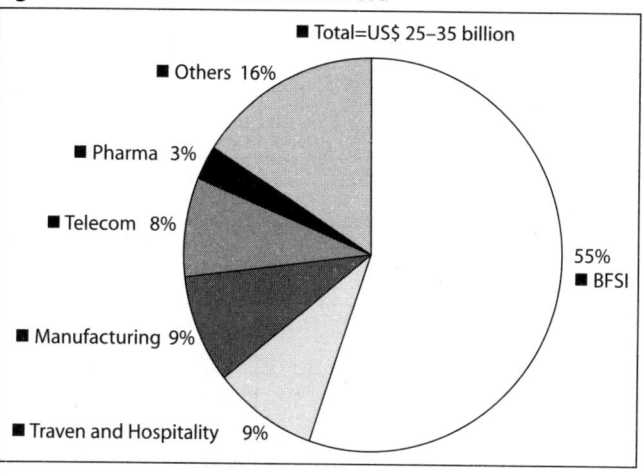

Sources: Gartner (2005); McKinsey Business Technology Office (BTO); McKinsey Global Institute; McKinsey Outsourcing and Offshoring Practice; *NASSCOM Strategic Review* (2005).

Table 1.3: Target Areas for BPO Firms in Financial Services

Sector	Established	Emerging
Banks and securities	Payment processing (cheques, credit and debit cards, ACH, SWIFT)[1]	Loan/mortgage origination[3]
	Issuing credit and debit cards/merchant acquisition[1]	Loan/mortgage servicing (establishing in some countries)[1]
	Cash management (as a commercial service to enterprises)[3]	Loan securitization[1]
	ATMs[3]	Research and credit/market analysis[2]

(Table 1.3 Contd.)

(Table 1.3 Contd.)

Sector	Established	Emerging
	Custody or trustee services[1]	Electronic bill presentment and payment (EBPP)[1]
	Trade support and settlement	Risk and compliance[2]
	Foreign exchange[1]	Trade matching[1]
	Fixed income[1]	Securities lending[3]
Insurance	(L&P) 'closed book' administration	Mobile and internet payments[1]
	(P & C) claims administration[1]	Business to business electronic payments[1]
	Policy processing[1]	Medical underwriting[2]
Common	Payroll[4]	Actuarial analysis[2]
	Benefits administration[4]	Loss adjustment[3]
	Customer service (contact centres)[3]	Recruitment[4]
	Education and training[2]	Real estate management[4]
		Record keeping[4]
		Facilities management (including business continuity)[4]

Source: 'BPO in Financial Services', *Gartner Report*, 22 July 2004.
Note: [1] = back office; [2] = middle office; [3] = front office; [4] = enterprise.

The size and quality of work here is indeed appealing and many companies have started BPO operations focusing only on the BFSI space.

The Global BPO Industry

It is evident here that the voice market continues to be large and constitutes about 40 per cent of the market (see Figure 1.4). The opportunity size is so large that it does not require any great analysis to boldly say that the next decade will see the BPO industry grow even more rapidly. Some optimistic estimates indicate that five years from today, the BPO industry would be larger than the IT industry.

North American companies have been very aggressive in promoting the outsourcing of business processes. Industry estimates indicate a growth in North American outsourcing from 39 per cent to 52 per cent between 2003 and 2006. Organizations are sending a clear signal that they recognize the high value addition that BPOs can deliver to their internal and external stakeholders. It is clear that the bulk of the work outsourced has been from North America. Having experienced the benefits of IT outsourcing, these companies have been fast to move and gain benefits from outsourcing business processes.

As of 2007, more than 80 per cent of the outsourcing of business processes to Indian companies has been done by North American corporates. Europe has been slow to start off. While banks and corporate houses in the United Kingdom (UK) have moved fast, the rest of western Europe has been slow in outsourcing. Stringent labour laws and stringent workforce protection cause challenges in countries like France to outsource work. These countries have the highest employee costs and benefits in the world, which is crippling their profitability and growth. The limited outsourcing that has taken place in western Europe has been outsourced to eastern Europe. But with an aging population, low childbirth, and high social costs, Europe would soon adopt and accelerate the BPO engine.

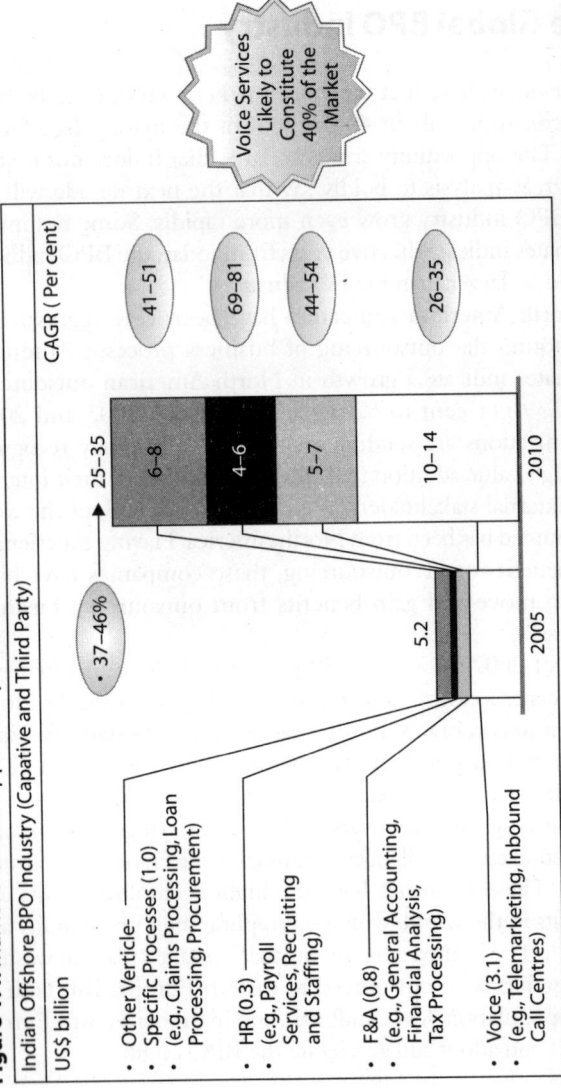

Figure 1.4: Market Size and Opportunity (in US$ billion)

Indian Offshore BPO Industry (Capative and Third Party)

US$ billion

CAGR (Per cent)

Voice Services Likely to Constitute 40% of the Market

• 37–46%

5.2 → 25–35

2005 2010

- Other Verticle-Specific Processes (1.0)
  (e.g., Claims Processing, Loan Processing, Procurement) — 6–8 — 41–51

- HR (0.3)
  (e.g., Payroll Services, Recruiting and Staffing) — 4–6 — 69–81

- F&A (0.8)
  (e.g., General Accounting, Financial Analysis, Tax Processing) — 5–7 — 44–54

- Voice (3.1)
  (e.g., Telemarketing, Inbound Call Centres) — 10–14 — 26–35

Sources: McKinsey Business Technology Office (BTO); McKinsey Global Institute; McKinsey Outsourcing and Offshoring Practice; Gartner (2005) database: NASSCOM *Strategic Review* (2005).

But the question looming large here is why do companies outsource their business processes? This was the subject of a survey done by *Gartner Dataquest* with customers in North America. Surprisingly, cost saving emerged fourth in the priority list.

The ability to improve service levels is a primary driver in large-business respondents' pursuit of BPO. For most companies, BPO is a service that helps them augment established services without necessarily supplanting them through wholesale swap-outs of people and technologies. As a result, large businesses cite the use of BPO to supplement staff or resources as averaging second on the list of drivers. Also, as many businesses grow, some perpetuate flawed processes over time, and BPO can improve processes merely as an alternative to the 'we've always done it this way' syndrome.

Here are the top reasons for large corporations to outsource their work (in order of priority):

1. Improve service levels.
2. Supplement staff/resources.
3. Focus on core business.
4. Reduce transaction costs.
5. Shorten implementation time.
6. Reduce implementation costs.
7. Gain process knowledge.
8. Re-engineer business process.
9. Migrate to new technology.
10. Introduce innovation.
11. Faster time to market.
12. Improve shareholder value.
13. Convert fixed assets to variable costs.

Since research companies look at BPO companies as distinct from the call centre business, there is no clear answer to what is the split between voice and non-voice operations within the BPO industry. One view would be that there are more customer support and helpdesk executives than finance and accounting (F&A) and back office support personnel in any company, hence the call centre pie would be much larger. We can safely concur that in terms of revenue, the contact centre business in 2007 would have generated a revenue of about US$ 30 billion globally, which is about 20 per cent of the total BPO industry. In terms of manpower, that would add up to 30–35 per cent of the total BPO industry.

Other key points about the BPO industry are:

1. The global BPO market is growing at a CAGR of 9–10 per cent.
2. Global offshore BPO is growing at a CAGR of 40–45 per cent.
3. The Indian BPO market is growing at a CAGR of 35–40 per cent.
4. Eastern Europe is fast becoming an outsourcing hub for the rest of Europe and is the fastest growing BPO hub.
5. China is making a slow start, but will clearly accelerate. Japan and Korea see China as a low-cost centre. China will experience the Mexico/Canada effect of near-shoring from these countries.
6. The largest scope for work is in the BFSI segment and this segment is expected to contribute to about 55 per cent of the total BPO industry.

The growth of the industry has had its share of debates. On the positive side, consumers have the advantage of low-cost real time services. It has created jobs and livelihood for people who otherwise would have struggled. It has also helped companies enhance their profits.

The flip side of this is poor service. Just think of the number of times you have banged your phone down in frustration trying to find out why the extra US$ 100 has been billed on your monthly phone bill and the person at the other end is not able to comprehend your problem. Managers complain of their inability to provide career growth and freedom from the monotony of repetitive jobs, which leads to high attrition.

Employees in the US are worried about work getting outsourced. This is because for every job that gets created in a BPO out-location, there is a job loss in the parent country.

In the last 25 years, manufacturing jobs in the US have seen a dramatic turnaround as they have fled to the shores of China and Taiwan. The knowledge economy boom of the last 20 years, be it in IT, telecom, bio-technology, or defence, have helped offset this loss of manufacturing jobs. While enough research and data shows that outsourcing helps companies, it takes time for the impact to reach individuals who lose their jobs and salaries.

When companies plan to outsource what is their top challenge? A *Gartner Dataquest* survey on large US corporations shows that that *loss of internal expertise* is a chief worry and challenge to outsourcing business processes.

Fifty-four per cent of large-company respondents cited it as the top inhibitor to outsourcing business processes. Large companies, because of their sheer size and scale of operation, almost universally have significant 'sunk costs' invested in building up their processes over time (inclusive of people and technologies). It is, therefore, understandable that loss of internal expertise would be a worry. In addition, such fears often include the loss of 'tacit' knowledge, that is, undocumented process knowledge carried intuitively by workers. The risk of losing tacit knowledge is especially acute in offshore BPO or in similar BPO contracts in which employees do not get transferred as a part of the undertaking.

Other top concerns voiced by customers include:

1. Can we automate using technology versus outsourcing?
2. Will outsourcing, especially to an offshore vendor, result in loss of control?

3. Will there be over-dependency? How do we manage disruption at the offshore site?

Surprisingly, job security is placed fifth in the list. But then this is the company's perspective and not the individual's perspective (see Figure 1.5).

The concern shared by many is that in the absence of the next big wave that creates jobs to substitute this loss, the livelihoods of the US back office workers could be under serious threat in the coming decades. This debate is now getting serious and is a key point in presidential election battles.

Notwithstanding this, BPO firms and call centres are here to stay and grow. It is a nascent industry and the focus and energy that is being spent on it will make it mature and stable as time progresses. Yes, there are challenging times for countries and companies that outsource and this will help them to further expand their horizon to newer fronts.

Types of Players

A very small percentage of the work has been outsourced to third-party vendors. Of the 30 million jobs in the global BPO market, less than 600,000 have found their way to India.

Wherever outsourcing has taken place, it has been mainly through captive shared services centres in a low-cost location. In 2006, more than 40 per cent of the Indian industry was accounted for by captives. Many North American companies have set up shared services centres in east Europe.

Shared services centres and captives are an extension of the company which is leveraging the low-cost structure of a new geography. The initial expansion always happens through a captive for experimenting with the new geography and understanding the cost structure, the rules and regulations.

Figure 1.5: Concerns of Large Companies with Regard to BPO

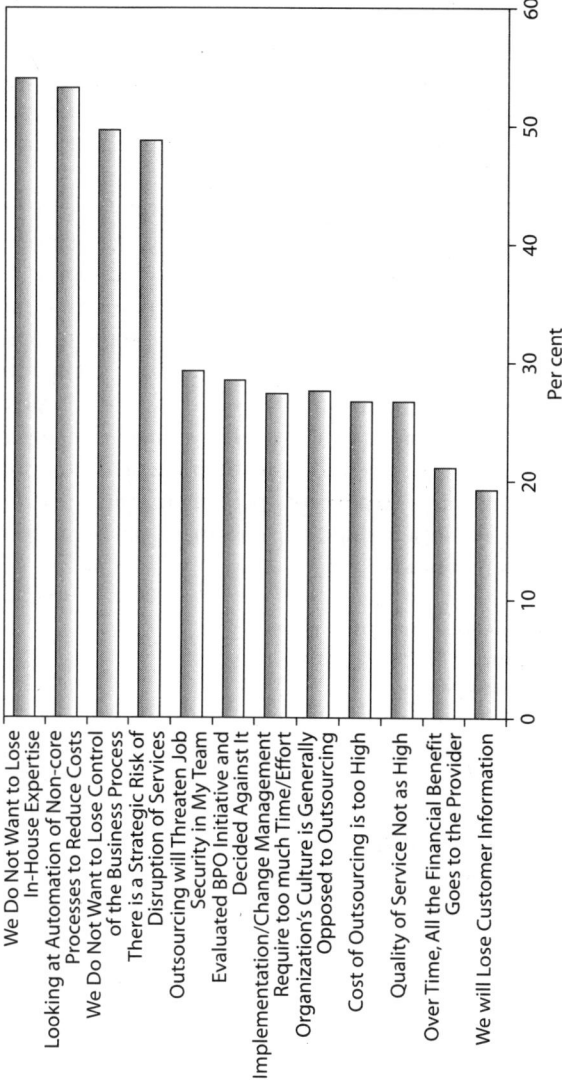

Source: *Gartner Dataquest* (October 2004).

Company executives who have moved from third-party service providers to captives indicate that the cost structure of captives is 30–40 per cent higher than that of third-party players. Having established their presence and seen the market situation, captives in the BPO industry will replicate the IT scenario by expanding future business with third-party players.

A third-party player manages the business end to end. From investing in infrastructure, hiring, to training, they manage the team to deliver the stipulated SLAs for the customer. They manage to scale up and scale down the operation within a short span of time as they can cross-utilize the people to operate business for other clients. Given the intense competition, customers have seen attractive rates from third-party players. Most third-party players have an operating margin ranging from 7–18 per cent. Industry leaders managing a tight shop would be operating with a 20 per cent operating margin.

Third-party outsourcing companies may again be categorized under different heads:

1. Stand-alone third-party players.
2. Integrated IT-BPO players.
3. Boutique shops.

Companies like ACS, Convergys, Teletech, Sykes, etc., are examples of large integrated BPO players. They operate at a global scale, have multiple centres across the globe, and many have revenues in excess of US$ 1 billion. They are mature companies with well-established processes.

Indian IT giants have also become key players in the BPO space—Wipro, Tata Consultancy Service (TCS), Infosys, Satyam, and Hindustan Computers Limited (HCL), have all started BPO operations and are in a ramp mode. Many of them have been acquiring smaller companies for accelerated growth.

Global consulting firms like IBM, Accenture, Capgemini and EDS form the last layer. Not only are they integrated IT-BPO players, but they offer a variety of services across the globe.

Genpact is trying to drive its growth the other way round. Starting as GECIS, the captive for GE, they became a third-party player, had a successful IPO, and are working towards building an IT business. They have had reasonable success, making them perhaps the first truly BPO IT company.

Boutique shops are specialized players offering services around engineering design, animation, specialized analytics, etc. They are small in size, work with limited clients, and have a large presence onsite.

A recent category that has been emerging is called managed captives. Also called BOT (build operate transfer), these are centres run with the infrastructure, look, and feel of captives, but the manpower, training, and managers are provided by the third-party players. This is an interesting trend and indicates that many companies still do not have full trust and faith to let go off their baby to third-party players.

Domestic BPO firms are centres that cater to the local market. Several banks, airlines, and telecom companies in India have set up domestic BPO units to cater to their local customers. This business has, till date, been ignored by the larger companies, since it is not very profitable. However, in 2007, the domestic BPO industry surpassed the US$ 1 billion mark in revenues, which has led many companies to start looking at this sector seriously.

These domestic BPO companies vary in size from 25 people to large centres with thousands of people. Twenty-five per cent of the domestic BPO centres are involved in outbound calls trying to sell credit cards and loans. The recent move by the Indian government to implement a do not call (DNC) registry will affect this business.

Companies like IBM Daksh, HTMT, First Source, and EDS MphasiS are serious players with the capability to grow in the

Indian domestic market. The quality of people working at these centres is a notch lower than those in international centres and they are paid 20–30 per cent less. The centres are located in small towns. Many of them employ people who speak the local languages. Since the jobs are day shift, many of the challenges associated with international call centres are eliminated. While there are 20–25 large BPO companies that employ more than 1,000 people, the Indian market has over 5,000 BPO players who employ anywhere from 25 to 20,000 people.

Vendor Selection Criteria

While selecting vendors, clients look at companies that have a track record of delivering good service. This is closely linked to the earlier survey result, where we observed that the top reason for entering into a strategic BPO relationship was improving customer SLAs.

The decision to outsource business processes is taken at a strategic level—it is a decision taken by the CEO with the full support and backing of the chief finance officer (CFO). These are long-term commitments and the partnership is sought with companies of repute and standing. The other criteria kept in mind while evaluating a partner are:

1. Financial stability.
2. Process expertise.
3. Industry expertise.
4. Cost per transaction.

Low cost is the fifth most important criterion in the list of priorities (see Figure 1.6).

However, the clearly measurable benefit from outsourcing clients is cost benefits and clients agree about this vehemently.

Figure 1.6: Criteria for Selecting a BPO Partner

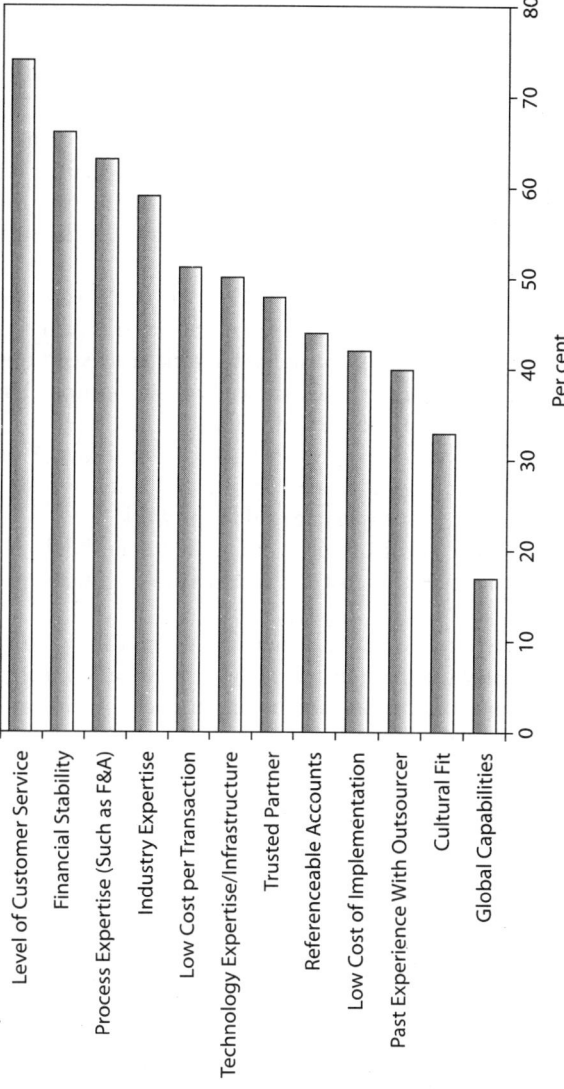

Source: *Gartner Dataquest* (October 2004).

Cost saving could be as high as 40–50 per cent. This is closely followed by productivity improvement and customer satisfaction.

These are important points from the context of Indian BPO providers who seem to have overlooked the importance of customer satisfaction and productivity, and position their value proposition primarily on cost savings. We will talk in more detail on the low-cost approach and its impact on the Indian BPO industry in a later section.

The contracts entered with BPO firms could vary. Most contracts are output based. The service provider is paid by the client service provider on completing work in a fixed time or on meeting certain thresholds of customer satisfaction. There are bonuses and penalties linked to this.

A simpler version is a contract linked to fixed fees. A third version could be payment based on time and material costs per hour or per day for people engaged in the work.

A progressive form of contract is called open book. Here the vendor recovers his cost and is paid a pre-negotiated profit margin.

Contracts tend to get re-negotiated every 18–24 months. With currency fluctuations taking away hard-earned margins, more and more companies are looking at pricing their services in the local currency rather than in euros or dollars.

BPO Valuations

Recent mergers and acquisitions (M&As) and IPOs have indicated that BPO valuations are significantly higher than their IT counterparts. This trend has resulted in many captives wanting to adopt a third-party model or to sell out.

A quick look at valuations indicates that BPO firms have valuations two-three times higher than that of their IT peers. If two companies with the same turnover, same levels of profits, one from IT and the other from BPO were to list on the same day (other things like brand, credibility, etc., remaining the same), the BPO unit would list at a higher price. This is an indication of the market seeing a better long-term potential for the BPO industry.

There has been a spate of IPOs and M&As in the BPO sector recently. With valuations hitting the roof, captives are selling off their units and making whopping amounts of money. The small players are finding it a challenge to run profitable units. Captives are selling in a hurry, fearing that valuations will drop. Three years back, captives accounted for over 70 per cent of the industry; the recent sale and conversion of GECIS and WNS to third-party players has changed the landscape to 50 per cent captives and 50 per cent third-party players. In the next five years, this could further change to 30 per cent captives and 70 per cent third-party players.

After WNS and EXL, Genpact was listed in the New York Stock Exchange (NYSE). In August 2007, Genpact listed at US$ 14 and accumulated over US$ 490 million. In October 2007, the company had a market cap of over US$ 3 billion and a price–earning (P/E) ratio of 147. This was with revenues of about US$ 600 million. At the same time, the Indian IT leaders—Infosys and Wipro—had a very different story to tell. Infosys had a market cap of over US$ 27 billion and a P/E of 28.67, while Wipro had a market cap of US$ 20 billion and a P/E of 27.

A third angle for comparison would be the US-based BPO giants. Affiliated Computer Services (ACS) is the big daddy of the BPO industry with revenues of over US$ 5.77 billion. The company had a market cap of US$ 4.92 billion and a P/E of 19.83 (in 2007) (see Table 1.4).

Sudip Nandi, the former chief strategy officer at Wipro, who had been instrumental in driving the 'string of pearls'

Table 1.4: Comparison of Companies

Company	Type	Revenues (in US$ billion)	Market Cap	P/E
ACS	BPO	5.77	4.92	19.83
Convergys	Call centre	2.85	2.33	14.08
Genpact	BPO	0.716	3.06	147.24
Wipro	IT-BPO	4.05	20.88	27
Infosys	IT-BPO	3.36	27.02	28.67
WNS	BPO	0.411	0.69	22.94
EXL	KPO	0.157	0.61	26.96

Source: Based on financial reports of the companies.
Note: Data as of October 2007.

acquisition strategy at Wipro, has been studying this trend closely. He feels that the short-term growth in valuations of Indian IT companies are muted due to the multiple headwinds that the business faces. These include appreciation of the Indian rupee, rising wages in India, the nearing of the end of the income tax holiday in 2009, softening of demand in the biggest market to name a few. The last 10 years have seen a rare bull run for these stocks and analysts probably see the best years behind them. It will require Herculean efforts to sustain the current valuations given the size of these companies.

BPO company stocks are getting picked up more by retail investors than institutional investors who are hoping that there could be another Infosys or Cognizant in the making. Investors see the BPO wave clearly lasting for another five years.

Leading analysts and NASSCOM predict that the BPO industry will grow faster than the IT industry. Some even believe that the growth of the BPO industry could be 50 per cent faster than that in the IT industry. The question on everyone's mind is can these valuations be sustained? Will IT companies spin off their BPO units as separate divisions and will captives continue to maintain a sell order? It will be interesting to see the trend in the coming years.

Recent M&As and IPOs have indicated that BPO valuations are significantly higher than their IT counterparts. This trend has resulted in many captives wanting to adopt a third-party model or to sell out.

Global Hot Spots

Given the size of the market and a large onsite business for BPO companies, the US is indeed the largest market for BPO.

India is the largest outsourcing market. China, Hungary, the Czech Republic, Costa Rica, the Philippines, Singapore, Vietnam, Ireland, Mexico, Central America, and Canada are other large markets. The latter countries are more of near shore centres feeding the large US market. A near shore centre offers proximity and low costs, making it an attractive value proposition.

The BPO industry started gaining momentum around 2000 in India, in 2003 in the Philippines, and is just about getting started in China (see Figure 1.7).

The cost advantage of Asian countries is compelling. Scale and size is helping them grow rapidly. India had already proven itself as an IT outsourcing hub. By exceeding revenues of US$ 5 billion in 2005, the Indian BPO industry has achieved in five years what the IT industry took over 10 years to achieve.

The advantage of a good system of English education has helped India and the Philippines to rapidly grow in the contact centre business. The 10–12 hour time differential with the US has also helped.

Figure 1.7: BPO Outsourcing Hot Spots

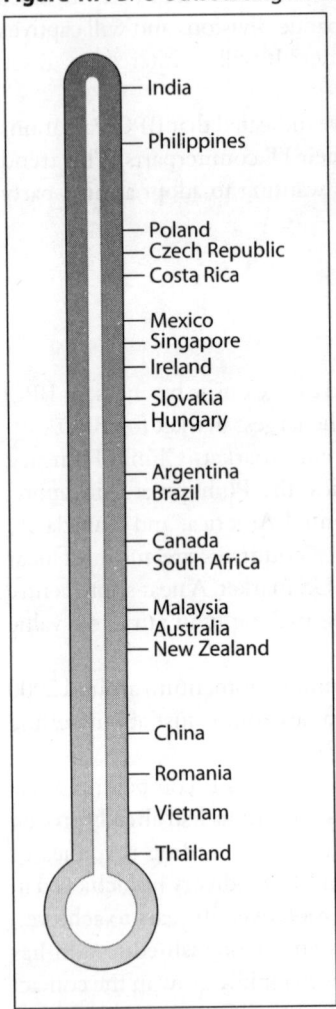

- India
- Philippines
- Poland
- Czech Republic
- Costa Rica
- Mexico
- Singapore
- Ireland
- Slovakia
- Hungary
- Argentina
- Brazil
- Canada
- South Africa
- Malaysia
- Australia
- New Zealand
- China
- Romania
- Vietnam
- Thailand

40

In the last few years, the growth of the Philippine contact centre industry has been phenomenal. This has attracted some of the leading players from India—Office Tiger, Sutherland, Genpact, Transworks, First Source, and even Infosys to set up base there. Having been an American colony, the Philippines has a strong foundation of English education. The challenge with the Philippines is that 90 per cent of the business is based in Manila. Other cities like Cebu, Clark, Davao, and Baggio do not have the necessary infrastructure and population to support a scalable industry. With less than 400,000 graduates every year, Philippines may find it a challenge to scale going forward.

Online performance management system removes subjectivity and brings in transparency. More humane and soft approach to business has resulted in the Philippines call centre industry maintaining attrition levels at 30–40 per cent lower than that in Indian companies. Attrition is the curse of the industry—it is like rust.

In the non-voice space, China is the country to look out for. A disciplined workforce, large number of college graduates, excellent infrastructure, and a friendly government makes China the ideal destination. Their cost structure is comparable and in some cases even lower than that of India. Japanese and Korean language proficiency is an added advantage.

Source: C.B. Richard Ellis release.

Given the higher cost structure of Shanghai and Beijing, the BPO industry is moving to low-cost centres like Dalian, Shengzhen, and Chengdu. The booming BPO industry in Chengdu has also attracted the attention of international players. In February 2007, IBM opened a new global delivery centre in Chengdu, its fourth in China after Dalian, Shanghai, and Shenzhen

Countries like Russia, Hungary, Romania, and the Czech Republic in east Europe are rapidly becoming the outsourcing base for Europe. Multi-language capability in French, German, and Russian in these countries makes it attractive. The cost structure is lower than that of west Europe.

South Africa is another emerging location—it has a large labour pool with multilingual skills. Proximity to the Middle East and Europe, and a deep cost advantage vis-à-vis the US and west Europe makes it an attractive option.

Every country has some level of presence in the BPO world. Whether it is Brazil or Mexico, Honduras or Ghana, the BPO wave is sweeping across countries and continents.

During one of his trips to India, Jean-Herve Jenn, the president of Convergys, indicated that rising costs and the burden of attrition did not make India look very exciting in the future. He mentioned that though India is the third largest centre for the American giant outside the US and Canada, he was not sure if it would retain the position down the line. He felt that India was the best option as of now, but for the future China looked more promising, as he felt that the Chinese were more committed and disciplined towards education and training. Although no single nation poses a threat to India's dominance, during the past two years, over 50 countries have emerged to cumulatively threaten its position in the BPO market. Industry experts estimate that India would grow, but continue to lose market share in the offshore BPO market to these new emerging players.

Evaluating a Global BPO Centre—Four Important Points to Consider

1. Educational hub and talent pool availability: Do not just look at numbers, look at quality. In India, for example, less than 15 per cent of the engineering graduates are employable. When you are setting up a centre you would like to expand it to a certain size over the years and look at talent that can help you expand and run a centre of 2,000–3,000 people with both new hires and replenishment.

2. Infrastructure: Connectivity with airports and roads, availability of backup power.

3. Local geo-political situation: Certain locations could have a higher degree of political unrest. Since BPOs need to run 24x7, disruptions through strikes would have an impact on business. One strike a quarter takes away four working days in a year. In a calendar year, after deducting weekend holidays and annual holidays only 250 productive workdays are available. Four additional days' losses would result in a 2 per cent productivity loss both in terms of revenue and profits.

4. Managerial talent also looks at being in growth areas. Across India, managers would prefer being in Bangalore, or Mumbai, or New Delhi, or Kolkata because of the growth opportunities that exist here. In the initial days it is a tough sell to convince people to go to smaller locations and it requires a lot of push from the local governments to make it happen. Look for a progressive stable government in the state, which welcomes investment.

Table 1.5: Leading Voice Players in the Global Industry

Megaproviders with Revenues Greater than US$ 1 Billion	Other Providers
Convergys, Teleperformance, Client Logic	EDS, West, IBM, TeleTech, Accenture, Sykes, ACS, Vertex, Sutherland, Genpact, Wipro BPO, 24x7 Customer, Sutherland

Source: Research conducted by the authors.

With a high of US\$ 44,516 in Denmark to a low of US\$ 2,489 in India, the variation in the salaries of call centre agents is large (see Table 1.6). As employees grow, salaries increase by 15 per cent year on year (YoY) in India. However, the entry-level salary has not seen much of an increase over the years. This is the basis for Indian companies maintaining their high profitability.

Table 1.6: Indicative Salary for Call Centre Agents across the World

	US\$	INR
Austria	16,075	643,000
Denmark	44,516	1,780,640
France	22,386	895,440
Germany	34,776	1,391,040
Israel	10,000	400,000
Netherlands	16,022	640,880
Spain	14,640	585,600
Sweden	30,375	1,215,000
Canada	40,000	1,600,000
Ireland	29,400	1,176,000
UK	27,300	1,092,000
US	35,000	1,400,000
Brazil	3,415	136,600
India	2,489	99,560
Poland	7,613	304,520
South Africa	11,029	441,160
South Korea	19,105	764,200

Source: 'International Perspectives on Management and Employment', *Global Call Centre Report* (2007).

Note: Entry-level salaries as of 2007. Currency conversion calculated at US\$ 1 = Rs 40.

What is Common across Global Call Centres?

Across the world there are a lot of similarities and some areas of differences between call centres. A recent survey of 475,000 call centre employees spread across 17 countries conducted by the Global Call Centre network in 2007 points to the commonalities and differences in the global contact centre industry:

1. The call centre sector is relatively young, with the typical call centre being 8 years old. Its growth is linked to the need for enhanced real-time customer service. Every successful company across the world has a toll-free number to sell products or to assist customers.
2. Call centres typically serve national rather than international markets. Eighty-six per cent serve their local, regional, or national market. This trend is more visible in developed economies. Emerging economies like India and the Philippines are predominantly hubs that service a global clientele. In 2007, while the Indian market grew very rapidly, the domestic market was less than 5 per cent of the total. This clearly indicates that this is an opportunity for the future.
3. Two-thirds of all call centres are in-house operations, serving a firm's own customers. Subcontractors operate the remaining one-third of centres. The final verdict on this would be interesting to see. In India, we have seen captives or centres under the direct management of customers having challenges in scaling up. The next phase of growth for companies from India and the Philippines would be in setting up near shore centres in the US.
4. Seventy-five per cent of call centres predominantly serve mass market customers, while 25 per cent serve business customers. Given the spread and diversity of processes and services, it is more difficult to serve retail customers.
5. A large proportion of call centres provide customer service only (49 per cent), while 21 per cent provide sales only, and 30 per

cent provide sales and service. Most centres primarily handle inbound calls (78 per cent), rather than outbound calls.

6. A typical call centre has a selection ratio of 20. In other words, one out of every five applicants is selected. This varies from country to country. India has a selection ratio of 8:100 while Korea has a ratio of 30:100.

7. Call centres are flat organizations, with managers comprising, on an average, only 12 per cent of employees. This varies from a low of 9 per cent to a maximum of 15 per cent.

8. Seventy-one per cent of the call centre workforce is female. Across the globe, women have a higher level of empathy and a non-threatening customer service attitude. In many cultures, they are not seen as the primary breadwinners and are resigned to the fact that a steady salary from a routine job helps the family.

9. Attrition in call centres varies from a low of 20 per cent in developed countries to a maximum of 100 per cent in developing countries.

10. Training duration varies across countries. In developed countries like the US and Canada, the duration of training is only 15 days. However, in countries like India, this could be as high as 8–16 weeks.

11. Temporary and part-time employees are the norm globally. Twenty-nine per cent of workers in call centres globally are temporary employees. In countries like Korea and Spain, over 50 per cent of employees are temporary. However, given the high duration of training, 100 per cent of the Indian workforce is permanent. TeamLease, India's largest staffing company, started a temping programme for the Indian BPO industry, but it failed miserably. They had to wind up their operations. Long training duration and very high attrition during training (over 150 per cent) makes it impossible for the temping industry to have a successful business model. Many call centres open up in college towns to attract part-time employees. This is a win–win situation for students and the call centre companies.

12. Performance monitoring and feedback mechanisms vary across countries. These happen on a monthly, bi-weekly, or weekly

basis. India has one of the toughest performance management criteria and performance feedback is given daily. A large component of the salary, sometimes up to 30 per cent, is linked to performance.

13. Variable pay based on performance is the norm for entry-level call centre employees. The average variable pay component in the salary package is 15 per cent. This is again split between individual and team performance. Eighty per cent of the variable pay is linked to individual performance and 20 per cent to team performance. In countries like India, where performance monitoring is very stringent, the variable component of the salary could be as high as 30 per cent.

Wipro's acquisition of Spectramind spurred the interest of IT majors. By 2003, all the leading IT majors had set up integrated or stand alone BPO divisions—Infosys set up Progeon and Satyam set up Nipuna. International players like Accenture, EDS, IBM, Hewlett-Packard (HP), and Convergys followed rapidly. This was followed by captive shops from Dell, JP Morgan, Deutsche Bank, and Fidelity. Today, the global giants dot the Indian BPO landscape.

The growth rate for the domestic industry has been faster, notching up over 50 per cent CAGR. The year 2007 will be a landmark year for the domestic BPO industry when it crosses the US$ 1 billion revenue mark.

While the Indian industry is growing rapidly, there is concern that India is actually losing market share. India commands less than 5 per cent of the global BPO industry and over 60 per cent of the offshore component. This 60 per cent is a drop from the 70 per cent it had a few years back. What this means is that while the pie is large, there are other countries that are getting their act in place.

What started in Gurgaon and New Delhi, rapidly spread to Bangalore and Mumbai. By 2004, these centres were beginning to saturate and expansion to second-tier cities like Pune

Hyderabad, Chennai, and Kolkata started happening. In the last few years, companies have started moving to third-tier cities like Jaipur, Bhopal, Vizag, and Chandigarh. The domestic BPO industry serving banks and telecom companies have started mushrooming in smaller cities (see Table 1.7).

Table 1.7: Average Number of Employees in Call Centres across Indian Cities

Location	Current Capacity (Number of Employees)	Monthly Hiring (Number of Employees)
New Delhi	50,000–75,000	4,000–5,000
Bangalore	50,000–60,000	3,500–4,500
Mumbai	35,000–50,000	3,000–4,000
Pune	15,000–20,000	1,750–2,250
Kolkata	7,000–10,000	500–1,000
Chennai	10,000–15,000	1,000–1,500
Hyderabad	10,000–15,000	1,000–1,500

Source: Research conducted by the authors.
Note: Data as of December 2007.

There is no dearth in the number of students who graduate from Indian colleges every year. But, only a small percentage of them meet the stringent eligibility criteria of the call centre industry.

India has an enrolment of nearly 10 million graduates spread across 341 universities and 16,000 colleges. This machinery produces over 441,000 technical graduates every year. However, the industry is able to employ less than 15 per cent of the non-technical graduates and 20–25 per cent of the technical graduates. This creates a huge problem of educated, but unemployed youth.

Every company wants to hire ready-made talent. The education system is not geared towards direct employment and a two-pronged approach needs to be made. State governments need to look at the education curriculum to make the college and university programmes more job oriented, while the industry needs to invest time and money on finishing schools. A little bit of polishing is all that it takes to make these graduates employable and that will go a long way in driving the growth and spiral effect of the boom.

An innovative way to fund these programmes would be to have a pay back for each student hired. This system is in place in business schools, but not in engineering and graduate colleges. The funds generated from such schemes can be used by colleges to redesign their course content and create laboratories to train students in industry-relevant topics.

This is an opportunity that some companies have started looking at. Aspire, a company started by Amit Bhatia (formerly with WNS), is looking at hiring and training people from smaller towns. They plan to set up a supply chain that feeds people from over 200 towns into their academies. The training conducted here is for two–three months and is customized to the needs of clients. In many cases, potential hires who fail to meet the initial threshold are ready to pay money to get trained. The rest is paid for by the hiring company. It becomes a win–win model for both sides.

Retail companies have gone a step further and are looking at monetizing recruitment. The entire cost of training is borne by the candidate and, in many cases, the training institutes are a sister concern of the firm that hires people. Even Kingfisher Airlines seems to have adopted this model by setting up a paid training academy.

A closer working between industry and campuses would also help. Some companies have started programmes where teachers spend six months at the company campus and get trained on specific programmes. They then go back to campus and the next batch of teachers go to the company for training. This gives the teachers a good feel of what is expected by companies.

Met to offer, a common ratio used in the industry, varies from 3–18 per cent. Captive multinational corporations (MNCs) paying high salaries have very stringent selection criteria. They make an offer only to 3 of the 100 people they meet. Third-party companies operate in a met to offer ratio of 8–15 per cent and domestic BPOs have a selection rate as high as 25 per cent.

Madan, the CEO of MeritTrac, has seen the landscape change over the years. MeritTrac has a structured way of defining voice quality (the parameters are fluency, grammar, voice clarity, and accent neutralization with a measuring scale of 1–5). A 4,4,4,4 score is the best and a 4,2,2,2 is a scrape through. Madan says that in 2000, at least 15 per cent of candidates would get a score of 4,4,4,4. Today, less than 10 per cent score 4,3,3,3. You rarely see a candidate with a score of 4,4,4,4 these days.

During the initial days of the BPO industry, students from the best colleges used to line up for jobs. It was a new industry and looked fashionable. Things have changed and many colleges do not allow BPO companies during campus recruitment.

The challenge for the non-voice business is not so acute and there is scope for rapid expansion in that space across metros and second-tier cities.

Niche talent for KPO and specialized fields like equity research, securities, insurance, and analytics are, however, concentrated in a few cities like Chennai, Bangalore, Mumbai, New Delhi, Hyderabad, and Kolkata.

Linked with talent availability is the rapid increase of real estate costs in metros. In the central business district of Mumbai, the real estate prices have quadrupled in the last five years. A company that would have leased a space at Rs 50 per square foot in 2002 would in 2007 have to renegotiate the lease at Rs 200 per square foot. Mumbai today has one of the highest office rentals in the world, comparable with London and Tokyo. This is a challenge for the growth of the BPO business and for companies thinking about expanding their business. Most will plan to dismantle their Mumbai operations and shift to less expensive cities. We already see this happening. A number of companies have already shifted their base from Mumbai to nearby Pune, and now pressure is mounting on Pune.

Lathika Pai used to run B2K, a BPO firm in Bangalore. The company used to provide technical support and was also expanding into non-voice areas like legal services, remote diagnostics, secretarial services, and the like.

Looking at the increasing cost of operations, Lathika took a conscious decision to sell her company to ALLSEC. Steep increase in the cost of staffing, real estate rates, coupled with lower rate realization because of competition and an appreciating rupee made her realize that sustaining the business would be a challenge.

With a good mix of voice and non-voice operations emerging as a business strategy for most companies, the next set of cities for expansion would be amongst those listed in Table 1.8. Each of these cities can support an employee base in excess of 10,000. An estimated 70 per cent of the BPO industry in these cities would be in the non-voice space.

Unlike Mumbai, Delhi, and Bangalore, centres set up in the smaller towns need to be smaller—1,000–1,500-seat centres with a hiring capacity of 100 per month for voice operations and 200–300 per month for non-voice operations.

There is a direct correlation between attrition and large centres. Smaller centres are easier to manage and have lower attrition rates. American companies have learnt this the hard way—rarely will you find a call centre with more than 1,000 seats in the US. Indian companies still seem to bet on operational efficiency by having 3,000–4,000-seat centres. This could be one of the reasons for the higher levels of attrition in India.

Table 1.8: Future Growth Cities

City	Suitability for Voice Operations	Suitability for Non-Voice Operations
North		
Jaipur	Average	Good
Chandigarh	Excellent	Good
Dehradun	Excellent	Good
West and Central		
Baroda	Average	Excellent
Nasik	Average	Good
Indore	Average	Average
Nagpur	Average	Average
Ahmedabad	Average	Excellent
South		
Coimbatore	Average	Excellent
Cochin	Average	Good
Mangalore	Average	Good
Vizag	Good	Excellent
Mysore	Good	Excellent
East		
Shillong	Excellent	Good
Siliguri	Good	Good
Jamshedpur	Good	Good
Durgapur	Good	Good
Ranchi	Average	Good

Source: Research conducted by the authors.

Most of these cities have a high literacy rate, many in excess of 70 per cent. There are certain geo-political constraints, which need to be considered. For example, companies have been hesitant about setting up operations in cities in West Bengal, the north-east, and Kerala because of political unrest in these areas. Customers avoid Gujarat because of its history of communal riots.

Durgapur is a classic example of a small city ready to scale up and meet the needs of a BPO city. An industrial city set up by B.C. Roy in the 1960s, it has a well-established steel industry, the anchor industry, around which numerous other ancillary units have come up. The town has excellent infrastructure and a good education base. It is a small town of 300,000 people spread over 30 sq.km on either side of the Grand Trunk Road. It is located close to Kolkata and has, in the recent past, seen a spurt in development activities. The cost of real estate is reasonable. In the past, people from Durgapur had to venture out to Kolkata to get jobs outside the manufacturing industry. Thanks to the telecom revolution, connectivity is a given today.

For setting up a simple 1,000-seat centre, the running cost in Durgapur would be 40 per cent lower than Mumbai or Delhi. This value proposition is already being experienced by a few early birds who have set up their domestic BPO centres in Durgapur.

There is a strong possibility that five years from now, the BPO industry would help in transforming Durgapur into a city like Pune.

There are hundreds of such cities waiting to be explored and the BPO industry is ideally suited to help them grow.

The only modification that companies will need to make when expanding to these cities would be to open mid-sized centres. A 750–1,000-seat centre would be the best bet. The cities are small, infrastructure is decent and affordable, and the talent pool is not very expensive. The revolution has not touched them as yet and they are eagerly awaiting the BPO boom.

Smaller centres are easier to manage. The Philippines has adopted this model very effectively. In Metro Manila, there are many companies that have four or five centres spread across the periphery of the city. Carol, CEO of the largest recruitment firm in the Philippines, says that this model has helped the companies attract people from across Metro Manila and the surrounding areas.

When organizations go on campus drives in smaller cities every year, they find a lot of people eager to join initially and make thousands of offers. However, only 40 per cent of these people join up for work and more than 30 per cent of them leave within 30 days.

This is especially so in the case of women who find it difficult to leave home and find a suitable place to stay in large cities. Paying guest accommodation and hostels are still not very structured. They are run by mom and pop shops and most parents are worried about the safety of their children. Staying with relatives is difficult; houses in metros are small and usually families are large and the living situation cramped. On a Rs 10,000 (US$ 250) per month salary, if you have to pay Rs 5,000 (US$ 125) per month just for accommodation, there is not much left to sustain a decent living.

Sai Babu, the head of sourcing at Wipro BPO has used his sales and marketing experience to come up with a productized version of campus recruitment. Tying up with universities and colleges, his team runs a Wipro BPO 'job fest' every week in small towns. The vice chancellor, college principle, the local press, and even local politicians of the town get into the act to welcome a giant like Wipro. The reception is fabulous and we see a flood of people. In Sripur, a small town 200 km from Aurangabad in Maharashtra, when a job fest was held, 1,700 people turned up for evaluation in two days. Sadly, less than 25 met the selection criteria. That is a met to offer ratio of less than 2 per cent.

Sai says that given the challenges in hiring in metros, this is the only way to go. It is hard work, but if you need to meet your numbers you have to go to smaller cities. What we need to also do is tie up with the colleges and provide training in the last semester to make the conversions higher.

Going to second and third-tier cities is clearly the need of the future. Companies like Infosys and Genpact have expanded to Jaipur, Bhubaneshwar, and Mysore. Many domestic call centres are coming up in smaller towns like Madurai, Tiruchi, Indore, and Nasik.

Most recruitment firms are exploring this opportunity actively. Senior executives from leading firms are setting up companies to tap this large talent pool. Finishing schools that can help increase the conversion rate will soon start opening in smaller towns and feed talent to companies.

Smaller cities have fewer job opportunities hence attrition will be low, salaries will be lower, and companies and employees will benefit. It is better for a person from Coimbatore to earn Rs 8,000 (US$ 200) per month and stay at home rather than earn Rs 10,000 (US$ 250) per month and stay at a hostel in Bangalore.

Dr Jagdish Sheth concurs and says that this is the trend in the US also. In a small town, the job of a teller in a bank is a career. People are happy and live a comfortable and respectable life.

Across the US, corporations have started mining smaller towns for their call centre operations. In 2006, Netflix opened its call centre at Hillsboro, Oregon. A city of 88,000 people, it is now home to four other major companies—Yahoo, Wells Fargo, Bank of America, and Farmers Insurance. A representative of the company says that real-life nice people are also nice on the phone. This fits in well with the culture and people see this as a career. Companies on their part have not set time limits for calls or the number of calls that need to be rushed per day as that would go against the culture of the people working here.

The BPO story is even going rural. Sai Seva is a BPO unit in Puttaparathi (a well known small town, known as the birth place of Sai Baba). The company was started in 2006 by four friends—Sai Narayan C.D.K, Sujata Raju, R. Prashant, and Prasad Ayyagari—all of whom worked with leading MNCs. The company was built on the fact that 8 million educated rural youth in India are unemployed. Given an opportunity they would prefer to be close to home and not migrate to larger cities.

The company has been able to successfully bid for projects from HDFC and Royal Sundaram. The cost of operations is half of that in a metro, and the quality of people is quite decent. The people recruited are trainable, the discipline levels are high, contentment is high, and there is hardly any attrition. Innovative initiatives like this will transform the landscape of India.

Growth has happened in a three-dimensional mode. Companies like Spectramind, Transworks, Daksh, EXL, 24x7, Customer Asset were BPO start-ups. Many of them were acquired—Spectramind by Wipro, MphasiS by EDS, Daksh by IBM, etc. 24x7 is the only BPO firm which still continues to grow rapidly and maintain its own identity.

The second set of companies were the IT companies which started their BPO divisions—Infosys set up Progeon, which later got merged as Infy BPO, Satyam set up Nipuna, TCS and HCL had their own BPO units. Initially, IT companies wanted to maintain a unique identity for their BPO units, however, in the recent past, the trend seems to be integration of the BPO unit as a business unit of the parent.

The third set of drivers were the captives. While companies like Dell, AOL, and HP set up their own call centre captives, BFSI players like JP Morgan, Fidelity, Deutsche Bank, and Standard Chartered set up large centres predominantly catering to the transaction processing business. Some captives like GECIS have become third-party players with a clear mandate to be more competitive and rein in the costs. Others like Citibank are on the verge of selling their majority-held captive BPO unit.

Today the industry landscape comprises 50 per cent captives and 50 per cent third-party players. Captives have a larger share of transaction processing work while third-party players have a larger share of the call centre business. With captives having a cost of operations estimated to be 40 per cent higher than third-party players, estimates indicate that future growth will be powered mainly through third-party players. Start-ups and niche players are finding it difficult to get the scale and cost advantage of leading players. Like in other industries in developing countries, the big will continue to grow.

Another interesting trend in the comparison between the IT and BPO players is that the top five players in the IT industry control greater than 80 per cent of the IT market, however, the top five in the BPO industry control less than 25 per cent of the BPO market. This trend is expected to change in the next five years and follow the IT industry pattern. A strengthening rupee and rapid cost escalation will result in the 'best of breed' with deep pockets surviving and thriving.

Positive Impacts

A 2007 report from CLSI ('Chain Reactions—Indian IT's Impact on Economy, Consumption and GDP', *CLSI Report*, February 2007) presents the interesting contribution made by the IT/BPO industries to the Indian economy. The IT/ BPO workforce in India accounts for only 3–4 per cent of India's organized work populace. However, this group will account for 13 per cent of incremental car demand, 20 per cent of incremental domestic travel, and one-third of multiplex demand. On an average, people in the industry expect their salary to increase at least six times over the next 10 years. Insurance penetration amongst this group exceeds 80 per cent while the country average is 5 per cent.

For every job in the IT industry, the surround effect job multiplier is 2.4+. For the BPO industry this would be 4+. What this means is that for every person employed in the BPO industry, there are four additional jobs created outside. These include people employed in various activities like office boys, drivers, security staff, training services, recruitment consultants, real estate agents, transportation companies, hotels, PC support companies, etc.—the list can go on.

If we assume that each one of these people supports a family of two, what it means is that for every BPO job created in the country, there are eight lives being nurtured and fed across the country. This would translate to over 4.8 million people gaining from the benefits of the Indian BPO industry. That is nothing short of a revolution—a fact that the industry needs to be proud of.

Expanding this logic, if the industry achieves a size where it employs 2.5 million people (from the global available BPO strength of 30 million) then the industry would support and feed over 20 million people. Now that is the population of Australia.

Till the early 1990s, the cities of Bangalore and Lucknow were comparable in all aspects. Both were state capitals, had good educational institutions, had peaceful environments, and were considered retirement havens. In the last 15 years, a huge divergence has appeared between the two cities.

The growth of the IT/BPO industries and the surround effect, explained earlier, have fuelled the growth and total transformation of Bangalore, while Lucknow has hardly changed.

At a conservative estimate, the impact of the BPO industry on the Indian economy can be summarized thus:

1. Total BPO revenues in 2007=US$ 7 billion.
2. Industry gross margin at conservative estimates=15 per cent.

3. Cost of running and managing a BPO unit that is ploughed back to the Indian economy = US$ 5.95 billion (that is nearly Rs 240 billion).

Success Stories

Let us now take a look at some real-life success stories from the BPO industry.

Success 1: BPOzitions

Prathap Reddy and Sanjay Mulay started a small IT training firm in Bangalore in 1997. Between 1997 and 2000, they expanded to recruitment and concierge services, and by 2000 were running a Rs 10 million business. In the year 2000, they expanded to BPO recruitment and also started providing accommodation and relocation services. The business grew rapidly and in 2004 their revenues shot to Rs 100 million. In 2004, they started operations in Pune and started expanding both the recruitment and accommodations business. In 2007, they notched up revenues in excess of Rs 300 million.

Today they run two companies—BPOzitions, a recruitment firm, and Satellite Living Solutions, an accommodation and relocation business.

They recruit over 300 people per month and own 145 apartments and 29 guest houses in Bangalore and Pune. The rentals for these service apartments vary from Rs 500 per night to Rs 10,000 per night. The high-end apartments have lounge bars and restaurants built in. The in-house spa compares with those in five-star hotels.

Prathap says that many of their high-end apartments have been booked by corporates for the next two years.

Prathap started this business when he was 18 years old. Today, at 30, he smiles when he looks back at the success and growth he has had, thanks to the BPO business. While they did not mention their profit margins, a service business like recruitment and service apartments operate at profit margins in excess of 50 per cent. It is amply clear to see what a successful business model they have set up. Here are two entrepreneurs laughing all the way to the bank thanks to the BPO industry.

Success 2: MeritTrac

Yet another outcome of the BPO boom is the success story of MeritTrac.

MeritTrac is India's largest skills assessment company. Founded by Madan, Murali, and Mohan in 2000, the company today employs over 450 people and provides services in 16 cities to over 200 customers. Their revenues are shared equally from IT and BPO assessments.

The company was set up on the following value proposition:

1. Assessment in mass hiring requires a process and needs to be treated like a core activity.
2. There should be no conflict of interest, hence the need to keep recruitment separate from assessment and training.
3. Services should be customized and scaleable to the needs of the customer.

The model was interesting and MeritTrac was successful in getting two rounds of institutional investments. In 2007, Manipal Education Services invested over Rs 500 million in the company.

Madan says that more and more companies talk to him on improving efficiency of operations. Recruitment and training across corporations function at efficiency levels lower than 50 per cent. There is a lot of scope to bring in predictability and improvements in the business. The road ahead is probably to look at end-to-end recruitment process outsourcing (RPO) services.

The talent pool is shrinking. In 2000, according to the founders of MeritTrac, they were able to select 15 people from every 100 they met. Today, that number has shrunk to less than 10. At the same time, the demand of the market has gone up over 10 times.

NASSCOM has been talking about a national registry for evaluating people for the BPO industry. This will eliminate repeated testing of a candidate by different companies. It would provide a score, something akin to GMAT or GRE scores, which can be used for a specified period.

MeritTrac has launched a similar programme called TracSkills. Given the huge demand for people and the complexity of assessments on similar lines by Indian BPO companies, MeritTrac expects TracSkill to simplify procedures for hiring in a standardized manner across BPO firms.

Success 3: Arun Kurup

Arun Kurup completed his engineering degree from a college in Thanjavur in 2001. He joined Bharti and then moved to Wipro BPO, New Delhi, in end-2002. At that time he just knew of Wipro being an industry leader in IT and had no idea of what a BPO was. Joining as an associate, he became a team leader in two years. He then applied for an internal job posting and moved to the supply chain business efficiency function in end-2005 as an assistant manager. His performance was superlative and in April 2007 he became a deputy manager. Today, Arun heads the central management information system (MIS) for people supply chain and manages a national team of 16 people. His team generates over 20 critical reports, which are reviewed by the CEO and the management team on a daily basis. Over the last five years, Arun has got four promotions and his salary has increased over 600 per cent. In December 2007, he married a colleague from the same organization. No industry in the world can have this type of growth in responsibility and remuneration for entry-level employees.

Success 4: Verifacts

Col. Swapan Bhadra is a distinguished army veteran who earned gallantry awards in the 1971 war. He retired from the army and joined the corporate world, and held senior management positions in TCS, Deutsche Bank, and Zee Telefilms.

Post 9/11, Col. Bhadra saw the immense need for background checks. What started with MNCs soon started expanding to Indian companies. Today it is not just the IT/BPO companies that insist on background checks, but manufacturing, retail, airlines, and every industry now insists on detailed background checks. It is a business that is over Rs 10 billion and growing by leaps and bounds.

Spotting this need, Col. Bhadra started Verifacts Services Pvt Ltd in 2005. What started in his study with hard work and dedication soon started showing results. Background verification is a tough job and clients insist on tough deadlines. India unlike the US does not have information stored online and this necessitates physical visits to the nooks and corners of the country to verify facts about a person's background.

In line with the growth of the business, Verifacts has grown astronomically. Between 2005 and 2007, his turnover has grown by over 400 per cent annually and he sees that trend continuing in the future. Today his is one of the biggest companies in this

61

space. He employs over 200 people and boasts of the who's who of the Indian IT/BPO industry as his clientele.

Success 5: Nikhil Patel

Nikhil Patel hails from Gandhinagar and migrated to Mumbai in 2000. He joined a driving class and got a license. Being jobless, he immediately grabbed the first opportunity that came his way and became a driver in a company that provided services to BPO companies. Within a year of working, Nikhil realized that the industry was growing and here was the scope to run his own business. He managed to take a loan from his village and bought a car. He engaged that car with the same contractor. He used to work three shifts and since he was driving his own car, he made the money to buy a second car in less than a year's time. His brother started driving the second car he invested in. Today, Nikhil has five cars and makes a monthly income in excess of Rs 100,000 (US$ 2,500). Thanks to the BPO industry and his spirit of entrepreneurship, Nikhil is a proud and successful businessman.

Success stories like these are common across the BPO industry and reflect the fact that this industry has touched the lives of people at the grass-roots level and helped them in a significant way.

CHAPTER 2

Changing Dynamics of the Indian BPO Industry

As mentioned earlier, the seeds of the Indian BPO industry were sown in the early 1990s. However, it was only from the early 2000s that the industry embarked on a journey that is making global news. The growth of the industry can be divided into three phases (see Figure 2.1):

1. Getting started and building on the idea.
2. Growing and consolidating.
3. Growing exponentially.

Between 2000 and 2003, the industry got started with a few start-ups. Companies were in a concept sell mode convincing US corporations to experiment with them. The focus market was purely North America. A lot of hard selling was required to convince large corporations to give critical real-time work to small start-ups. The carrot in front of customers was the significant cost reductions—labour arbitrage was the key driver. There was an enormous effort to train people to speak

Figure 2.1: Changing Dynamics of the Indian BPO Industry

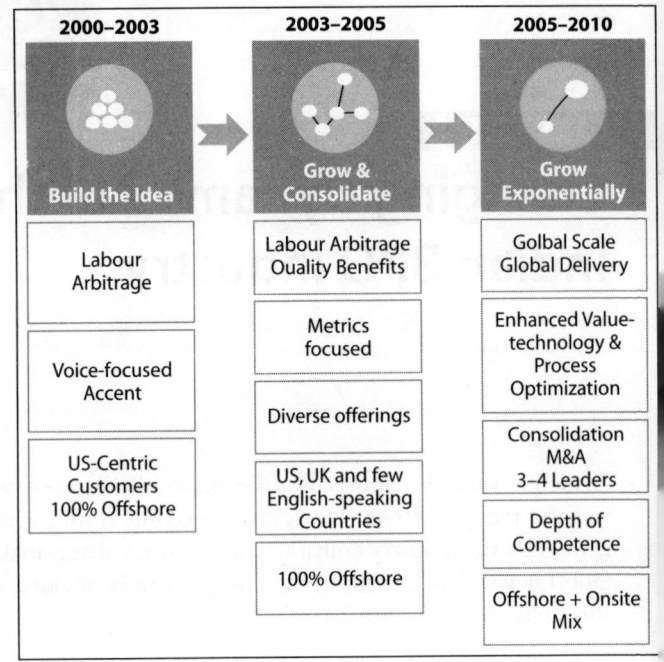

Source: Research conducted by the authors.

like Americans. Companies had set up shop in New Delhi and Bangalore. Business was 100 per cent India-centric.

In the second phase (2003–2005), the industry consolidated and grew rapidly. India as a BPO destination had been established. Along with costs, the benefits of quality and standardization were also available to customers.

Customer engagements grew larger; companies started diversifying their offerings from stand-alone services and started experimenting with focused horizontal and industry solutions. The focus of the industry, which initially was only on the US market, expanded to also include the market in UK. Industr solutions, quality tools, metrics, LEAN, Six Sigma benefits, and the like were increasingly being shared with customers in this phase. The focus was not just on labour arbitrage, but also on productivity. Companies started looking at non-linear growth. Business was still 100 per India-centric, but centres of operation expanded beyond New Delhi and Bangalore to Mumbai, Pune, Kolkata, Chennai, and Hyderabad.

We are now in the midst of the third phase. The industry is growing rapidly and exponentially. All the business lines across industry verticals like banking, airlines, telecom, manufacturing, and health care are well established. There is both span and depth of expertise in the Indian industry. Deal sizes are getting larger; integrated IT-BPO deals are common. Quality systems are robust. Most players have opened centres in smaller third-tier cities in India; larger players have opened global centres in east Europe, the Philippines, and China. The market is abuzz with mergers and acquisitions (M&As) and captives are losing direction.

As the BPO industry has traversed this journey, there are a few interesting changes that have happened along the way. Many of them have been subtle, but when we look at them in a consolidated manner, they are significant changes.

The 'Big Daddies' Take Over from Entrepreneurs

The first few years of the twenty-first century belonged to young entrepreneurs who had the dream of kick-starting a nascent industry. Probably for the first time in Indian history, we saw a number of able entrepreneurs starting BPO organizations and helping them grow rapidly. Raman Roy of Spectramind, Sanjeev Agarwal and Pankaj Vaish of Daksh, Nagraj and Kannan of 24x7, and Ganesh of Customer Asset, are all successful entrepreneurs who started new companies and helped them grow or sold them off successfully. Not only did they create wealth, but thousands who worked with them saw big bucks for the first time. It looked as if a Silicon Valley revolution was about to begin. Sadly, however, that trend does not seem to have continued.

In contrast, we do not see too many high-profile BPO start-ups today. The big guys—Genpact, Wipro, Tata Consultancy Service (TCS), Infosys, WNS—clearly are on a trajectory where they will soon control more than 75 per cent of the Indian BPO market.

The only exception to this is 24x7 Customer. They are the only BPO with revenues in excess of US$ 100 million which has plans to grow on the foundation built over the last seven years. The founders are clear that the game is just beginning.

While there are smaller companies like MarketRx and μSigma that have emerged, given the size of the industry, one would have liked to see more active action in the BPO start-up space.

A 2001 National Association of Software and Services Companies (NASSCOM) BPO summit attracted people from all walks of life—doctors, accountants, lawyers, even farmers—all eager to see what the BPO industry had in store and how they could ride the wave. The NASSCOM BPO summit in 2007 was attended by the chief executive officers (CEOs) and executives of the big BPO companies.

With no dearth of venture capital (VC) funding for good ideas and people, it is surprising to see the wave of entrepreneurship dying down.

Perception of the Industry has Changed

The BPO industry started in the backdrop of the dot-com boom-to-bust cycle. People who joined the industry in 2000–2001 were skeptical about the long-term growth and stability of the industry.

The positioning of the industry was also built along these lines. Advertisements for employment talked about a party lifestyle. The positioning was fun. Long-term career was never a core selling point. The value proposition was to attract the highly educated unemployed. They were typically the offsprings of white-collared executives. Students from the best colleges used to line up for jobs.

While the perception created in the initial years still lingers on, the approach taken in the last few years has been radically different. At US$ 7 billion, there is no doubt about the growth trajectory of the industry. Questions about the long-term viability of the industry are no longer raised.

There is a mad scramble for talent, and companies and industry bodies are working at positioning BPO firms as offering a long-term, fast-track career. People joining the industry are from small towns and for most of them this is their first job. They are the sons of blue-collar employees, they are from small colleges, and many are not even graduates.

Right-selling the job is a positive step that the industry is taking and augurs well for the future.

Quality of Workforce

Madan Padaki is the CEO of MeritTrac, which is India's largest skills assessment company. MeritTrac was started in 2000 and Madan has been working with large BPO firms, helping them select the right candidates. MeritTrac has a tool called SET which helps categorize people on the basis of their communication skills. As per the tool, a score of 4,4,4,4 is the best and a score of 4,3,3,2 is just about acceptable in the BPO industry.

Madan says that in 2000 they used to meet a lot of candidates with a score of 4,4,4,4, while today it is a rarity to spot even a handful. Across the country, less than 15 per cent of the candidates who they assess have a score of over 4,3,3,3 (MeritTrac assesses over 50,000 candidates every month). Companies that never accepted scores below 4,3,3,3, earlier are now accepting candidates at levels of 4,2,2,2, and spending additional time in training them and helping them attain speed.

This seems to be the situation across the country across all companies. As the demand for talent has shot up astronomically, the talent being churned out from colleges is not meeting the mark of the BPO industry. The industry on its part has been slow in working with colleges to help them train and groom students in order to meet the mark.

In the initial days, an interview for a BPO company used to take 15 minutes; today there are over 50 tests that are administered. Voice tests, typing tests, accounting tests, Excel skill tests, data entry tests—you name the skill and there is a test for the same.

As companies go deeper into the country's hinterland to hunt for people, the quality of scores will continue to drop. This is one concern that should not become the Achilles heel for the industry.

Levels of Engagement

Engagement levels in a BPO firm can be in the transactional mode, relationship mode, or partnership mode (see Figure 2.2). In the initial days, the engagement was purely in the partnership mode.

Customers wanted to make a success of the engagements—they worked hand in hand with the companies. Be it in setting up the infrastructure, or conducting training programmes, the customer's involvement was total and it was not in the spirit of micromanagement, but in the spirit of partnership. The

Figure 2.2: Levels of Engagement

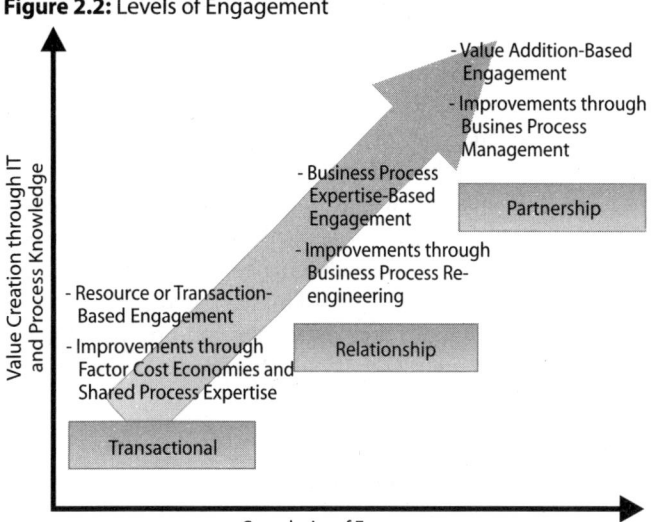

Source: Research conducted by the authors.

quarter business review (QBR) involved the equal sharing of information and best practices.

Things today are at best between the relationship mode and transactional mode. It is more about ensuring that service level agreements (SLAs) are met and contractual terms are enforced. The spirit of cooperative working is getting minimized.

Positioning of Captives

Over the years there have been three distinct positionings of BPO firms—small domestic BPO firms, the large third-party service providers, and the captives.

Captives were the people with fancy offices and perks. Their salaries were 40–50 higher than industry levels. People saw it as a logical progression to move from a domestic BPO organization to a third-party firm to a captive firm.

In the last one year, the direction of captives has become confused. Most of the leadership cadre working in captives are not sure if the business will grow or if the captives will be sold since valuations are high. The performance of captives and their delivery of services have been lagging behind and are not at par with those of third-party players. This has raised questions from corporate offices about their efficiency and productivity. For the first time we are seeing people think twice before joining a captive as a reverse trend has started.

No Longer Metro-centric

The first phase of growth saw BPO companies being set up in the National Capital Region (NCR), Bangalore, and Mumbai. In the second phase, the BPO industry spread to Chennai, Pune, Hyderabad, and Kolkata. The third phase has seen the industry's expansion to Jaipur, Bhubaneshwar, Baroda, Ahmedabad, and Coimbatore.

A combination of cost and search for talent is driving companies deeper into the country's hinterland.

Expansion is taking place not just in India, but also globally. Most of the big players have set up global centres in Hungary, Poland, the Philippines, and China. They are looking at aggressively building up these centres.

The Recruitment/Training Game Scales New Heights

The scale and challenge of recruitment and training has gone up 10 times in the last few years. Not only have the numbers gone up, so has the complexity.

The hiring process today consists of a battery of assessment tests, background and reference checks, medical checks, and an intense round of training before the candidate can become productive.

The cost of hiring, which used to be Rs 4,000–5,000 (US$ 100–125) in 2000 is touching levels of Rs 15,000 (US$ 375). Companies are picking up students in their second year of college and are even ready to accept undergraduates who are older than 18 years. The upper age limit has been increased by many companies to 55 years to attract retired people.

The training function is faced with the challenge of making these people adaptable to the BPO world given the strict eye on costs. The training timelines are stringent.

Every CEO mentions that the challenge for growth is not inflow of business, but lack of resources to keep up with increase in business. Every business unit head states lack of resources as the reason for not being able to meet his growth of numbers.

When we reflect, the changes that the industry has experienced in a short span of seven years have been numerous. This is what makes the BPO game exciting and pulsating. Employees and managers have deftly managed these changes and steered the industry to growth and glory. This is the key ingredient that creates structured chaos.

CHAPTER 3

Managing a BPO

Industry Dynamics

An MBA decided to go to the countryside and set up a farm. He was convinced that all that he had learnt in business school (B school) would help him improve productivity and run the farm as a role model for others. He called a meeting and issued a dictat to all the chickens that in order to bring about predictability in sales they would need to deliver two eggs every day. Anybody failing to do so would face severe consequences.

Not used to such pressure tactics in the countryside, the chickens got scared and started delivering eggs. There was one chicken, which for two consecutive days delivered only one egg. This chicken was called up for a performance review and strongly pulled up. Towards the end of the blasting, the MBA farmer asked the chicken what the issue was, to which he replied, 'Sir I am a cock. I tried my best but could come up with only 1 egg.'

Figure 3.1: Work Pressure in a BPO

The BPO industry is no different. Stringent performance management and the perpetual need for people are the key drivers of the BPO industry.

A chief executive officer (CEO) of a leading BPO company once remarked, 'I see the entry-level workers of the BPO industry as battery packs. Once they are drained out we must replace them.' That is the mindset which has caused serious damage to the industry. With the industry just having touched the tip of the iceberg, its future potential and growth should not be marginalized due to such short-term focus.

Think of a chariot driven by four horses and marshalled by an expert driver. Does it remind you of the Gita? Well, there is a symbolic relation between this and a BPO company. Like Lord Krishna, the driver of this chariot, the CEO of any BPO firm, has to be an astute businessman—shrewd, knowledgeable, dextrous, intelligent, and hard working. He also needs to have guile and the ability to be ruthless.

The horses pulling the chariot are the business units or the operation teams that keep working 24x7. Sourcing and training are the wheels of the chariot—they constantly keep moving ensuring that the company has the right talent to run its business effectively. Compliance and quality are the whip used by the driver.

Ask any CEO managing a BPO company and he will say it is no different from war. In this world of structured chaos, there is always scope for improvement at every step.

The primary problem for the industry is—people! Good affordable people are becoming extinct. With attrition in the industry hitting the roof, the need for good, sincere, and affordable people is a perennial one. A CEO at a BPO company once jokingly commented, 'Don't be surprised if you very soon find a board outside our campus saying "Trespassers will be hired."' BPO companies always have vacancies. This is the only industry where anybody with diverse skills walking in will be entertained and evaluated.

The biggest challenge in a BPO is it works in seventh gear. You always need to get things done yesterday. And this sense of urgency is capitalized by many to their advantage.

Anjan Guha is a 28-year-old. He completed his bachelor of art (pass course, a two year graduation course) from North Bengal University. His scores did not get him an entrance to the three year graduation programme. He joined a captive call centre as an agent in Kolkata. Within 18 months, he moved to another large captive BPO in Delhi as a group leader, worked there for two years, joined a third multinational corporation (MNC) BPO and moved to the transition team where he was involved in multiple projects. Anjan seemed to be a right fit for a manager in the transition team—a right fit in a Rs 800,000–1 million (US$ 20,000–25,000) per annum salary range. Anjan was a smart guy and was going to get an offer letter when he blurted out his expectation of Rs 2.6 million (US$ 65,000) per annum. The rationale behind it was, 'I am currently paid a salary of Rs 1.4 million (US$ 35,000) per annum. I am expecting my annual salary hike next month. That would be a minimum of 20 per cent. I am expecting my promotion in three months, which would entail a 20–30 per cent hike in salary, and if I want to move I would expect a 20–30 per cent hike in salary after taking into consideration the earlier two increases. That would amount to: Rs 1.4 million * 1.2 * 1.2 * 1.3 = Rs 2.62 million (US$ 65,000) per annum.'

Anjali Gupta was another candidate for the role of a process head in the Kolkata operations of a BPO firm. She was 35 years old, a single mother with a masters degree in English literature. She had worked as an assistant professor for eight years in a college. She joined an MNC BPO company in Kolkata as a trainer and within two years moved to an operations job. She then changed two jobs—one in Mumbai and one in New Delhi. She was an assistant vice president (AVP) earning Rs 1.8 million (US$ 45,000) per annum, managing operations for a domestic call centre process. In the five years she had been in the BPO industry, her salary had gone up from Rs 300,000 (US$ 7,500) to Rs 1.8 million (US$ 45,000) per annum. She was clear that she wanted to move to Mumbai. The cost of living in Mumbai was 30 per cent higher than Kolkata. She was also expecting a hike of 20 per cent in her salary in a month's time and would be keen to move if given a 20 per cent overall hike and an additional 30 per cent hike to cover Mumbai's cost of living. So her working was: Rs 1.8 million * 1.2 * 1.3 * 1.2 = Rs 3.4 million (US$ 85,000) per annum. When quizzed on what was the talent growth she had in her for demanding a salary increase of 500 per cent in five years, her answer was simple and clear, 'I don't know how long the industry boom will last. Today people are ready to offer me the salary I ask for. I have a daughter to look after. I don't know if I will have a job five years from now. My friends are getting this salary—what's the harm in asking. If I ask for Rs 3.5 million (US$ 85,000), we will close at Rs 3 million (US$ 75,000).'

I meet at least four candidates every week to keep in touch with the market realties. Cases like these are common every day. Salary and designations in the BPO industry have lost significance. Human resources (HR) managers have given up their attempts at trying to maintain parity. There is always a new customer, a hot skill, or an urgent requirement, to justify the need to pay astronomical salaries—and people are needed now. Pay off the notice period, let us get the person working from tomorrow is the dictat we often hear.

The biggest challenge for people is at the entry level and in middle management. The hottest segment today is the bracket comprising people with 5–12 years of experience—right from a manager to an AVP. They form the backbone of any company and salaries here are increasing at 30–40 per cent year after year against an industry average of 15–20 per cent.

Another interesting incident took place in January 2007. A leading BPO company hired an excellent manager as the regional head of sourcing at a salary of Rs 1.5 million (US$ 37,500). He was head of HR for a smaller firm, had 12 years of experience, and was keen on a larger role. He was sold the job and the responsibilities and joined at the same salary. He did a superb job and had a huge impact on the company in a very short time. Six months later, the company wanted to hire another regional head. All the candidates short listed by the company were in a Rs 1.8–2.4 million (US$ 45,000–60,000) salary range and their credentials and quality were at par or below those of the first regional head. Following this, the regional head's salary was corrected.

Being a large company, parity was maintained and good talent was retained. However, many companies that do not have strong HR practices are no longer able to afford parity. Given the rapid changes, it is difficult to benchmark salaries every quarter. The result is that BPO companies have a wide range of salaries. We have seen companies where you have AVPs with similar skills in similar roles in salaries ranging from a mere Rs 1.2 million to a whopping Rs 2.5 million. This sort of diversity is unheard of in any other industry.

Not just the voice business, but salaries for fresh chartered accountants (CAs) and cost accountants are skyrocketing. At the CA campus recruitments in September 2007, offers were made in the range of Rs 400,000 (US$ 10,000)–1.2 million (US$ 30,000) per annum. Over 101 companies hired nearly 1,800 candidates in two days. The average salary was Rs 600,000 (US$ 15,000) per annum and the highest salary was Rs 1.2 million (US$ 30,000) per annum. ICICI Bank alone picked up 300 candidates. IT/BPO companies like Tata Consultancy Service (TCS), Genpact, Infosys and Wipro BPO were also prominent recruiters.

This is good news for CAs who for years were positioned a rung below engineers and MBAs. In small town Durgapur, where I grew up, society was harsh and a bachelor of commerce—B.Com. was spelt out as 'Budhi Kom' or 'less brains'. The cream always choose to be engineers or doctors. The rest got bachelors of science (B.Sc.) degrees. Those who did not gain admission to a B.Sc. course went in for a B.Com. degree and then struggled through to chartered accountancy.

While the IT boom saw a dream run for engineers, the BPO era is opening up new frontiers for accounts and finance professionals. Not only do they get off to a good start, but the knowledge process outsourcing (KPO) business pays top salaries all along the way. There are many examples of candidates with five years of work experience earning Rs 2–2.5 million (US$ 50,000–55,000) per annum. Attrition in KPO firms is beginning to raise its head, with job-hopping becoming quite frequent. It is a simple question of demand and supply, and the rapid growth of KPO will accelerate this trend.

How do you run a business where the attrition is anywhere from 50–100 per cent, the salaries are rising at 15–20 per cent year after year, and the compound annual growth rate (CAGR) stands at 35–45 per cent? People who have seen both the IT and BPO industries say that if the IT business runs in third gear, the BPO business runs in seventh gear.

The complexity and challenge of a BPO is higher. This means that BPO salaries are higher at middle and senior management levels. 'It's like being paid a hardship allowance when you are posted at a difficult location like Siachen', says the HR manager of a leading firm.

Organizational Structure of BPO Firms

The structure of a BPO organization would be similar to most other services firms, however, the roles and responsibilities, and importance of certain functions would vary. Here is a bird's eye view of the different functions in a BPO firm, which will help new employees to plan and charter their growth path (see Figure 3.2).

Figure 3.2: Organizational Structure of BPO Firms

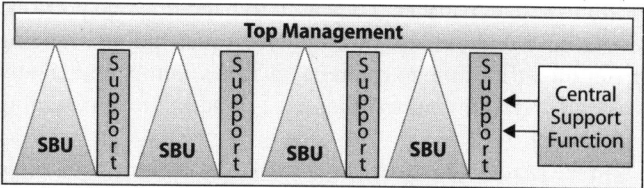

Source: Research conducted by the authors.
Note: SBU—strategic business unit.

In most organizations, the sales, finance, marketing, and HR functions would report into the CEO, while operations, quality, compliance, information system (IS), and technology would report into a chief operating officer (COO).

While each function has a critical role to play, the HR function is perhaps the most crucial link in this people-centric business. Attracting and retaining talent is the foundation for growth and companies that have addressed this have grown rapidly. Successful BPO firms are clear leaders in people engagement. The culture is driven from the top. These companies have the capability to grow rapidly and have strong systems to support them.

Given the dynamism and the need of BPO firms, successful HR professionals have applied innovation and marketing to drive new engagement models. They have evolved a new HR mantra for the BPO industry—by engaging and being a one point of contact for people issues they have made a huge impact. They are empowered and work with passion to make a difference in the day-to-day business. Their sense of empathy is high. They identify problems and work proactively. They realize the need to equip themselves with marketing and finance skills to be effective in their job.

The HR industry is going through a change. Across business schools, the smartest prefer jobs in finance or marketing. The talent pool getting attracted towards HR is getting smaller and smaller. In the factory era, the HR manager was called the administrative manager. They used to handle a large portfolio covering a wide aspect of employee touch points, ranging from the office time to cafeteria, facilities, compensation and benefits, recruitment, training, etc., in addition to managing the unions.

In the factory where my father used to work, only two people had the authority to fire employees—the managing director and the personnel administrative manager (the HR manager of the factory). Today, the role of HR is diminishing. While the intention is to focus and develop human capital, many HR organizations have not been able to do so.

Across companies, the line managers have taken away a large part of the role of their HR counterparts. Given their importance and complexity, sourcing and training have been spun off as separate functions and administration and facilities are run independently. What then is the job of HR? The HR department needs to do more than make policies and run surveys.

There is an identity crisis brewing among many HR managers across BPO firms, especially those who are not well-equipped to handle the needs of the day. Employee branding, fun at the workplace, higher levels of engagement, being the spokesperson for employees, and fighting for their cause are clearly areas that beg for attention. These require innovative leaders with good communication abilities. The search for good talent is frenetic here also.

Transaction to Transformation

Moving from transaction to transformation is a journey that most HR managers in BPO firms need to make.

The workforce in a BPO unit undergoes high stress. It comprises very young people. The negative aspects associated with the BPO industry are largely correlated to the behaviour of these very young people. The point that needs to be debated is whether these negative aspects are a problem of the BPO industry per se or more a problem of hormones.

There are challenges because of the nature of the business. BPO firms are not dens of vice. HR in a BPO organization has the unique challenge of addressing these issues. Running a counselling programme, having an effective sexual harassment committee, ensuring transparency in movement of people between different roles are all very important. Training young 23-year-olds to be effective team leaders and managers is not a cakewalk. No other industry will have a team leader managing a group of 10–12 people.

The change in the role of HR from having to manage labour issues in a factory to managing an intelligent workforce in an IT/BPO has been rapid. The HR approach needs to change in line with the changing business. Innovation is key in terms of designations, salary structures, and retention bonuses. Out-of-the-box thinking is the name of the game.

Sourcing has moved from HR to sales and marketing professionals. This has been a silent and rapid change. For a profession that is so large and critical, there is no structured college or MBA programme that specializes in training candidates on the challenges of mass recruitment.

The head of sourcing has one of the toughest jobs in the industry. Hiring thousands of people month after month is mind-boggling. To this when you add the issues of assessment, medical and background checks, document filing, and channel management, it can make the most stable of people feel dizzy. Most people burn out in the function after 18–24 months.

The biggest challenge in sourcing is not just meeting your hiring numbers, but getting the right quality of people. The sources for hiring are basically three:

1. Consultants who contribute to 50–70 per cent of the hiring.
2. Employee referrals, which contribute to 20–40 per cent of the hiring.
3. Walk-ins, job fairs, response to advertisements, which result in another 10–15 per cent of hiring.

The ratio varies across cities. The dependency on consultants in the voice business is very high. In a mature market like

Mumbai or New Delhi, consultants would contribute to 70 per cent of the hiring. In the non-voice space, direct hires and employee referrals would be as high as 70 per cent. Hiring for the non-voice sector is not as challenging as it is for contact centres where decent communication skills are a must.

Industry veterans say that the bar for communication skills has been drastically lowered since the initial days, yet the numbers are so large that we are not able to catch up with business requirements. Even customers agree that our focus should be on problem resolution and not on accent.

With hiring and attrition being a challenge in the call centre business, companies have started focusing on the non-voice market. Attrition in the non-voice sector is 15–30 per cent and is comparable with the IT business. The size of the non-voice business is large and growth in this sector is two–three times larger than in the voice business. Talent for the non-voice business is amply available even in third-tier cities.

There are many placement consultants who have become millionaires in a short span of time supplying thousands of people to hungry companies. The average payment per hire is Rs 10,000 (US$ 250), but in cases of dire need, companies are ready to shell out even Rs 20,000 (US$ 500) per hire. At middle and senior level, the consultant's fees can be as high as 16 per cent of the annual cost to company (CTC) while large established players doing targeted searches would charge upwards of 30 per cent of the CTC per hire. Consultant payouts are linked with a retention clause.

There have been instances of scams in hiring and senior executives in leading companies have lost their jobs. There is easy money and no tight controls. Many consultants are known to call the same candidate after the retention period is over to place him elsewhere.

There is variation across countries. In the Philippines, a market that opened up after India, the dependency on channel is far less. Most of the hiring happens through portals and direct walk-ins. Less than 20 per cent of the hiring happens through consultants. The same is the trend in China also.

Employee referral schemes vary from company to company. Payments are in cash or kind varying from Rs 3,000–10,000 per hire at the entry level. This is an attractive scheme and many employees make a regular income in excess of their salary with referral payouts.

Job fairs are of great help to prospective clients, but it helps companies, which have higher salaries to attract the best of talent. Like IT companies, BPO companies have started massive campus recruitment plans. This is a good step towards strengthening the recruitment process. Most companies have a clear strategy to increase direct hiring.

Hiring from campus, second-tier cities, job fests, city recruitment centres, and attractive referral schemes are the way to go. The role of applied marketing in the sourcing team will increase as budgets will be spent in direct hiring rather than for consultant payouts.

But what should be the ideal size of the sourcing team in a BPO firm? The answer to this is directly linked to the type of people you are hiring and the location where you are present. In first-tier cities, in an international third-party BPO firm, a team of 20 can hire about 300–350 people per month.

What should be the structure of HR? Should it be the traditional integrated function comprising recruitment, training, and core HR, or should it be split into two or three separate functions? Companies have tried out different models to achieve efficiency and each model has its own set of advantages and disadvantages.

Many traditional HR managers strongly feel that sourcing and training are part of HR and should not be segregated. Identifying people in line with company values, inducting them, training them, mentoring them, and helping them to grow is an end-to-end responsibility of HR.

The other large function meshed between sourcing and operations is training. Training in BPO organizations can be split under four heads:

1. Communication or what is called voice and accent (communication tool kit).
2. Voice and floor coaching.
3. Process training.
4. Behavioural or leadership development.

The training programme for a new hire would last about three months. The voice and accent training programme is complex and requires customization for each geography being catered to, the US, the UK, Australia, and New Zealand being the predominant markets.

Training throughput is a cause for concern across companies. It varies from a low of 45 per cent to a high of 75 per cent. Training throughput is a simple ratio which measures the total people hired to those taking calls on the floor post-training. For example, if 100 people are hired and 50 take calls three months later, then the training throughput is 50 per cent.

The investment made in training is high and over a three-month period companies would spend about Rs 65,000–80,000 (US$ 1,625–2,000) in training a candidate.

Training departments are either run separately or integrated with operations. Like a chief training officer (CTO), the concept of a chief learning officer (CLO) is slowly gaining ground. Just like sourcing has been spun off from HR, corporate houses across the world are looking at how training can be effectively utilized to enhance productivity and run like a business with measurable output.

Training attracts a lot of people from operations. It is seen as a logical growth path for good agents.

The finance function helps a company control costs and keep a close eye on the bottom-line. In many BPO firms, CEOs have started using finance more effectively in managing costs. It is common to see finance teams involved in price negotiations with customers and creating innovative pricing models with a basket of currencies to avoid currency fluctuation losses.

Quality works closely with operations. Many of the manufacturing concepts of quality like LEAN have found their way to the BPO industry. Given the metrics that are used to measure different parameters (one company had over 210 reports generated every week on Excel worksheets), one of the key deliverables of quality is to create simple dashboards and help in driving the customer satisfaction (CSAT) curve upwards.

Umesh Vyas has been associated with many Indian BPO firms in their quest for quality. He feels that an obsession has gripped the Indian BPO industry. It is the obsession of managing individual performance through metrics. Although measurement per se is useful, some of the individual measures used are as reliable as rolling a dice. Unwisely used, numbers can create a tyranny, without improvement. Unless the focus is quickly shifted to the process and the system, current performance management is likely to turn into a spectre that will haunt the industry for years to come.

Let us consider the measurement of quality and examine what is happening. Quality is measured through monitoring. Each individual is monitored about 1–10 times a month. Each transaction monitored is scored. Individuals are given feedback based on these scores. These scores are used to evaluate performance. Rewards or punishment follow.

There are many quality standards and approaches adopted in BPO companies. While having a certification may not help you to get business, not having a certification may be a good reason for a propsective client to reject your organization. Certification is a useful way to advance your contact centre career, or evaluate how your centre stacks up against your peers. There are several quality certifications applicable to the BPO/call centre world. Let us take a look at some important ones:

1. ISO 9000: International Standards Organization (ISO) 9000 series, a European standard, is an international set of documents on quality assurance, written by members of a worldwide delegation known as the ISO/Technical Committee 176.

   The ISO 9000 series consists of five documents; three core quality system documents, that are models of quality assurance, namely, ISO 9001—model for quality assurance in design/development, production, installation, and servicing; ISO 9002—model for quality production and installation; ISO 9003—model for quality assurance in final inspection and test; and two supporting guidelines documents, namely, ISO 9000 and ISO 9004.

2. COPC-2000: This stands for Customer Operations Performance Centre. The COPC-2000® Standard was written in 1995 by a core group of users of call centre services and associated distribution fulfilment operations, including representatives from American Express, Dell Computer Corp., Microsoft, Novell, L.L. Bean. COPC is the world's leading authority on customer contact centre operations. COPC-2000 is used to improve customer service. In India it can cost anywhere from Rs 200,000–250,000 million (about US$ 50,000). It takes about a year to get the COPC-2000 certification. The adoption rate for COPC-2000 is much faster in India than other countries, which is a very good sign.

   The COPC mission is to develop and drive initiatives that support superior performance in customer-touch intensive environments, as measured by the criteria of customer service, customer satisfaction, and operation efficiency. These initiatives are developed and implemented in collaborative, consortium environment, which includes practitioners from both external and internal customer service providers (CSPs), outsourcers, industry suppliers, and other industry experts. Today, COPC audits organizations for compliance to the COPC-2000® standard; conducts benchmark reviews of call centres and fulfilment centres, using the standard as the organizing methodology for the data collected during the course of the review; consults with call centres and fulfilment centres on operational performance improvement; consults with purchasers of call centre and fulfilment services on strategic alternatives for outsourcing, including how best to select and manage suppliers; provides industry-wide forums, such as conferences, workshops, and facilitated user groups, to foster an atmosphere supportive of high levels of customer service.

3. BS7799 security standard: BS7799 is the most widely recognized security standard in the world. Although it was originally published in the mid-1990s, it was the revision of May 1999 that really put it on to the world stage. Ultimately, it evolved into BS EN 15017799 in December 2000.

   BS7799 (ISO 17799) is comprehensive in its coverage of security issues, containing a significant number of control requirements. Compliance with it is consequently a far from trivial task, even for the most security conscious of organizations. This website is intended to help address this issue. It will introduce the main sections of the standard, as well as a number of methods and resources to help you tackle it more efficiently.

   Achieving compliance with BS7799 is a substantial task. Assessing compliance levels for information systems, and then creating/implementing the necessary plans to become fully complaint, can by a very intensive process indeed. However, with the correct approach and method this effort can be minimized.

World of Operations

The world of operations in a BPO firm has some similarity to the world of manufacturing. The work is repetitive and monotonous. Delivery requires high levels of rigour and discipline. The quality standards that are set are very high—if you lose a customer you rarely get him back.

Infrastructure

Infrastructure is a critical link in every BPO firm. Since the work is done real time, the infrastructure needs to support that. A backup for a backup is the name of the game. Constant connectivity, transportation to pick up and drop thousands of employees, 24x7 cafeterias, robust security systems, and in-house medical services are all mandatory requirements in a BPO organization.

Transportation

Transportation in a BPO is a complex job. Across India there would be over 25,000 cabs operating, shuttling people in and out of offices round the clock. Getting people to come in on time, designing security systems, ensuring compliance of the systems are crucial elements. Most of the work is outsourced and it becomes difficult to manage and monitor cab drivers from varied backgrounds. Checking on their background, conducting their medical checks on a regular basis is important for the safety of employees. However, this is easier said than done. Most companies leave this job to the cab agencies, who do not have the system and the rigour to implement these measures.

Drivers of BPO cabs come from villages. They are not attuned to driving on city roads. They toil for long hours and many earn measly salaries of Rs 3,000–4,000 (US$ 75–100) per month. They are penalized with deductions if they are late in picking up or dropping clients. This results in stressed out sleepy drivers stepping on the accelerator and, hence, many accidents. It is common to see at least one accident every week, and most of them are fatal. (Everyday there are 350 fatal road accidents in India, but it is accidents related to the BPO industry that get prominent coverage by the press.)

The insurance that is paid to the employee's family in such cases varies from Rs 100,000–200,000 (US$ 2,500–5,000). It is hardly a remuneration that can compensate families for the loss of their near and dear ones. Many of the unfortunate employees are young and in their first jobs. They come from middle-class families and are breadwinners.

BPO services are perishable. Being real time, if you lose a call you lose money. Loss in connectivity, employees reaching office late, and any natural calamity can result in loss of business.

90 Information Systems

Information systems in most BPO firms are struggling to keep pace with the rapid growth of the industry. Many companies operate their systems through spreadsheets. Applications that exist are disparate and not connected.

Integrated enterprise resource planning (ERP) systems are a must for large operations. Lack of this limits the success of many companies, especially those wanting to expand globally. Systems bring in transparency—calculating your leaves, incentives, time offs, CSAT—many of which is today done manually by managers and team leaders. Manual intervention brings in subjectivity and this in many cases is the cause for resentment and attrition.

The rapid growth of the non-voice business has brought about the need for tools and platforms. There is scope for automation of work in a data entry/transaction processing environment. Companies which can develop these platforms stand to deliver higher value. This is an area for focus across companies. Many Indian BPO firms are on the lookout to acquire platform BPO units. Many such companies exist especially in the health care business.

Even in functional areas like transportation, training, and assessment—there is a need for technology adoption to attain non-linear productivity. The industry has been slow in responding to this need.

Compliance is an absolute must. BPO firms work on real-time customer data—confidentiality and privacy are high priority. When any company outsources work, there is a diligent evaluation of the security and compliance framework.

The Indian BPO industry has seen a few instances of financial frauds. The industry as a whole is very stringent about this and deals with it in the toughest manner. It is a question of survival for the industry and thus no chances are taken.

All these functions put together comprise less than 15 per cent of the workforce in a BPO. Operation comprises the remaining 85 per cent. Over the years, a structure has got institutionalized in this large-scale operation.

The ideal way to structure operations is along industry and business lines. A strategic business unit (SBU) is a building block. Each SBU serves a certain business and there is commonality of customers around the business unit (BU) customers. Each BU is structured around customers/process and has support functions embedded in it.

The levels and hierarchy in a BU varies according to operators—captives tend to have four or five layers while some large third-party players have seven or eight layers.

What is the ideal structure of a BU? How many people should a team leader or unit lead manage? What should be the focus area of people across all levels? Let us get a perspective on these issues and explore possible solutions.

Ideally an SBU should not exceed 2,000 people. Increasing it beyond this number would lead to challenges in managing it effectively. Each BU should have its own dedicated support functions and operate as a mini-company. The support functions would draw help from a central support team.

Most companies have a seven-layered structure within a BU (see Figure 3.3). We feel that this is overkill, leading to a lot of overlap. Being clear about your deliverables is the key to success in a high transaction environment. What will work more efficiently is a simple four-layer structure.

Figure 3.3: Levels in a BPO

Current Set-Up: Too Many Layers. Clear Deliverables at each Layer Need to be Defined to Avoid Replication of Jobs.

Manufacturing Set-Up: Four-Tiered Structure is Ideal and has been Implemented by some BPOs.

Source: Based on research conducted by the authors and their discussions with Takao Kasahara, managing director, Streamline Strategy.

Note: GM—general manager; SDL—senior delivery lead.

The team leader (TL) is the most critical layer in the structure. Most TLs manage 10–15 people, while ideally each TL should manage five–seven agents.

The ratios are typical for the voice BPO sector and can change dramatically for the non-voice business. In the non-voice business, the spread can be larger—one TL for 20 associates and one manager for 10 TLs.

The key to success is to make the job simple. If the job is simple, errors will not happen, it will be consistent, and fast. The TL should help the agent and not be loaded with reports and management information system (MIS) work that needs to be the ownership of the manager. This four-layer model will ensure high productivity and deliver quality on the floor.

Across the operations structure, the TL is the most important layer. A TL is typically a 23–24-year-old and manages a team of 12–18 people. He is a first time manager and the world at a BPO firm revolves around him. Let us look at some of the activities that a TL carries out during an average day:

1. Starts the day by preparing for the pre-shift huddle.
2. Conducts the huddle and briefs team members on job expectations, events in the company, internal job postings, change in transportation, etc. (Most BPO firms do not give their agents email addresses and hence the TL becomes a one point of contact for any information.)
3. Distributes work and administers login.
4. Monitors calls.
5. Coaches his new team members.
6. Takes part in operation reviews.
7. Conducts training.
8. Joins in meetings which plan for get-togethers/outings.
9. Prepares daily reports and presentations.
10. Attends review calls with manager/customer.
11. Is involved in appraisal/disciplinary action discussions with HR.
12. Works out the variable pay calculations for team members.
13. Prepares the stack rankings.

From an execution and operation angle, the TL is the core for the successful running of a BPO unit. He has the maximum span of control and the largest set of deliverables.

Looking at the crucial role of a TL, OnTrack, a company started by Ravi Venkatesh, has started a training programme that addresses the requirements of a TL. It trains and prepares a TL to be an effective manager. This is a unique customized programme and companies that have used OnTrack's service vouch for its effectiveness.

Ensuring that the CSAT dashboard remains green is the primary objective of the operations team. Agents have variable salaries and a portion of their salary is benchmarked against their CSAT scores. *Stack ranking* is a common tool used in the operation floor. It is a method by which people are ranked on their CSAT scores and the same is publicized daily. Bottom rankers are given a chance to improve their scores, but after periodic warnings if they do not do so their jobs are terminated. It is highly debatable if stack rankings are the best way of driving performance on the floor. The practice is established and seems to be prevalent across all call centres in the country.

Work in a BPO firm is monotonous—90 per cent of the job is repetitive. The challenge is how it can be made exciting. Making the job exciting is the first step towards making a value proposition for a BPO career. There are many people who have stayed on in the industry and have loved their jobs. Based on their experience with several BPO firms across the country, the management team at OnTrack has identified the following focus areas that could help BPO employees look at the positive side of their job:

1. Enrichment: Doing the same thing repetitively without knowing the science behind it can become very boring. Therefore, the idea is to seek external or internal inputs to discover why things are the way they are. For example, a frontline BPO employee could find out why there are so many metrics. What do they mean? How are they related? Why are they important to the client? What are the metrics in other processes? Why are they

different across processes? Similarly, they could discover answers in other areas, for example, what kinds of reports are produced? What do the fields in them mean? Who produces them and what can we understand from them? A frontline employee could also find out about the other functions in his process, discover what QA is all about, what workforce management is all about, and why there is a CSAT lead.

The number of answers to discover is literally infinite. Another way to find enrichment is to read up on topics related to the work. Such topics can be found in books, websites, journals, etc. Some people who continuously engage in this process will probably not find their job boring because every day will be different.

2. Depth: Another method to keep the excitement of the job alive is to get into the depths of the function. For example, an associate in a process that deals with accounts payable, could go into the depths of the domain itself (for example, invoice processing). He could also go into the depths of the large number of variations in the types of job processes for the client. Similarly, an agent in a technical support process could go into the depths of the functions of his process. These endeavours would make the agent an expert in the process.

3. Contributions: Some of the people who continue to remain excited about their jobs engage in a high level of contribution towards the job. These could be in the form of taking initiatives, lending a helping hand to the boss/colleagues, or to volunteer for tasks. One can come across numerous instances of people taking initiatives to improve process training, increase contribution to the knowledge base, improve quality or customer satisfaction, or any other form of process improvements, etc. Volunteering to resolve problems also helps make a job enjoyable (for example, helping clear up huge queues of work, volunteering to perform root cause analysis to identify a problem, etc.). Volunteering to help in other functions/departments also keeps the job enjoyable. For example, an agent in a BPO company wanted to move to a role in the HR department. This was proving to be difficult because of the non-existence of a formal lateral

movement process within the company. So he decided to volunteer his free time (on one of his off days) to help out some people in the HR department on some odd jobs. During this time he became familiar with most people in the department, including the head of HR. When the time came for the HR department to recruit a person, they obviously chose this agent, who was already familiar with them, and had built up his equity in the department by volunteering his time.

4. Professional interactions: Interactions with peers within and outside the company at a professional level help to foster interest in one's job. For instance, it would be very interesting to note how people from other companies are addressing a work-related problem that one might be currently facing. These interactions could happen in person (for example, through friends) or online. There are numerous groups on the internet where people discuss various issues at a professional level. Another way to foster such interactions, is to contribute to a newsletter or a magazine and then seek feedback

5. Experiment within tolerance levels: There is an old saying 'if you always do what you have always done, you will always get what you have always got'. Therefore, if the job seems to be boring, then it is time to change something in the way we do the job. One can always experiment, within tolerance limits of course, by tweaking a few components of the job. For example, a customer support executive could experiment on ways to build better rapport. To do this, he would need to change something in the way he normally speaks with a customer. For instance, he could read up the latest in entertainment news from websites such as MSN.com and use that knowledge in his conversation with his clients (for example, 'did you see the Oscars last night?'). Or he could choose a completely different technique, for example, speak to a friend in the collections process and ask how they build rapport with customers who they have to convince to pay up.

6. Building relationships: Another great way to remove the monotony from the job is to build relationships with a variety of people. These are those people who we would not normally

interact with. For example, a BPO associate might interact 70 per cent of the time with his colleagues, 25 per cent of the time with his TL, and only 5 per cent of the time with others (including managers, people from other functions, etc.). If he took the initiative to take a bit of his time and allocate it to interactions with other people, he would give himself a chance to build completely new relationships with a variety of people. A key success factor for people in any company is the number of relationships they build horizontally or vertically in their organization. Again, such endeavours keep the job interesting.

In the end, each individual's attitude towards his/her job will determine how exciting or boring they find their job to be. No one can tell an individual how to develop an interest in a job. For example, when a manager assigns a variety of tasks, some individuals can regard it as regular work. On the other hand, initiatives by oneself will be viewed as exciting because it comes with a higher sense of ownership.

Voice versus Non-Voice Operations

The world of operations is very different for the voice and non-voice sectors. Call centre employees have high-pressure jobs, but the minute they walk out of the office they can forget their work. There is no baggage that they carry with them. Less than 10 per cent of the calls are monitored, so if they make a mistake, they need to be unlucky to get caught and many get away with it. The very nature of their work makes them extroverts, confident, and the training in accent does bring about a swagger and style.

The profile of people entering the finance and accounts, KPO, industry-specific transaction processing sector is very different. They are by nature serious. They look upon the job as the first step in their career towards becoming a professional in that industry. They are keen on getting trained and certified to enhance their knowledge. Everything that is done in transaction processing has a trail. A delay, or mistake, gets tagged to you immediately.

Assume you are working on a banking, finance, security, and insurance (BFSI) process and are to close an account/deposit/investment on a certain day. Suppose you take it easy and miss out on the deadline. If the interest rates go up the next day, there can be a huge loss to the bank. A lot of actions are dependent on stock markets, foreign exchange rates, inter-bank rates, and the Federal Reserve rate, which vary by the second. The cost of an error in such a situation can be very high.

Designations

Asians, and especially Indians, are highly designation conscious. Growth is associated with your designation and the number of people reporting to you. People move between jobs for higher designations and better salaries. The BPO industry has capitalized on this. Designations in BPO are highly diluted. Getting a fancy designation in a BPO is a lot easier than in any other industry. Do not be surprised to see a candidate with 10 years of work experience carrying the tag of a vice president (VP). The associate vice president (AVP) designation was introduced in the country by the BPO industry.

One of the large companies had 21 VPs in HR and over 500 AVPs. People with seven–eight years of experience were designated as AVPs and their next promotion would be to the position of VP. This works as a retention strategy as an AVP, who is effectively the middle management layer, stays put in the dream of becoming a VP while if he leaves and joins a company outside he becomes a GM.

In the long run, this may backfire, as people will not find career growth. If you grow from a manager to senior manager to AVP to GM and find that you are still doing the same job, you will soon question the designation tag. What this means is that over a period of time, the pride associated with the designation will cease to exist.

Any job is a combination of three things:

1. Job role.
2. Designation.
3. Salary.

In a mature industry, all three are linked together. This model helps to create robust career growth for individuals. Designation changes only with a quantum change in job role. Growth and success are not necessarily measured by your designation. People can grow as specialists and earn high salaries.

The Attrition Bug

Why do people join a BPO company? It pays better than most other industries, has a glamour quotient, the quality of life is great, you get picked up for work and dropped back home, and there is always one party starting before the other ends. So why do people leave it?

There are different ways of reporting attrition. Most companies are defensive and report data that is lower than actual. There are different measures of reporting attrition:

1. Attrition of tenured associates: These are people who have been taking calls for three months. This is in the range of 30–40 per cent.
2. Attrition of people post training: This is in the range of 60–70 per cent.

3. Attrition in the first three months of training: This varies between 75 and 150 per cent.

If you total this up end-to-end for an average call centre, the attrition would be between 80–120 per cent. Companies having large non-voice operations would report lower attrition since non-voice attrition would be below 30 per cent. However, even leading KPO companies are concerned about the 30 per cent attrition, a figure that has shot up drastically, thanks to the burgeoning demand and numerous companies being set up.

It is a demand–supply situation and everyone seems to be going after ready-made talent. A market report on career opportunities in India's KPO sector predicts that if attrition in the KPO industry goes up, the industry will suffer and not be able to reach its growth potential.

Many entry-level agents quit because of salary—a 20 per cent hike in salary for joining another company when you have been in a job for only six months is a carrot too tempting to resist.

The entry-level salary for an undergraduate or a fresh graduate would be about Rs 125,000 per annum, that is, about Rs 11,000 per month. Post tax and deductions, the take-home pay would be about Rs 8,500.

There is an eternal debate on salaries. Are call centre agents paid in excess or is it the requirement in today's fast-growing economy? There are two sides to this coin:

In 1980, a person holding a masters in technology (M.Tech.) from the Indian Institute of Technology (IIT) would earn Rs 1,800 per month, which in 1990 was equivalent to Rs 3,500 per month. A doctor working in a government hospital earns less than Rs 10,000 (US$ 250) a month. An assistant professor at IIT earns about Rs 250,000 (US$ 6,250) per year as a starting salary. A qualified engineer who has cleared the Indian Telecom Services (ITS) examination would work in BSNL, MTNL, or DOT at an entry-level salary similar to that of an IIT professor. And most commerce graduates working in a small chartered accountant's (CA) firm would earn Rs 7,000–8,000 (US$ 175–200) a month even after three–four years of work experience.

If you look at it from this context, the salary of a fresh associate in the BPO industry does look attractive. Add to this the fact that since pick up and drop facilities are provided and subsidized food is available in the cafeteria, you have an incremental saving of Rs 5,000 (US$ 125). Then it really looks like an unfair advantage and some would even say that the BPO industry is a pampered industry.

The second perspective is contradictory to the first. Given the fact that salaries comprise 40 per cent of the cost of a BPO firm, and over 80 per cent of this is paid out to entry-level workers, what is the justification for BPO companies handing out such huge entry-level salaries? Does higher salary reduce attrition? Logic would say yes, but the reality is very different. We have seen companies that pay Rs 18,000–20,000 (US$ 4,500–5,000) per month as starting salaries, which is 30–40 per cent higher than the industry average, but they have attrition rates as high as 100 per cent.

While salary is a cause of concern in an economy that grows at over 9 per cent, the real issue is relative salary. If you see your batch-mate, or peer earning a higher salary, you might get disgruntled. And that acts as the trigger to look out for a better pay packet in a different company. It is more of an ego issue in the peer group to which you belong.

Dr Jagdish Sheth, professor of marketing at Goizeuta Business School, Emory University, has done extensive research on BPO companies across the globe. His view is that the call centre industry across the globe has high attrition rates. In the US, high school dropouts are the ones joining the industry. In India, it is college graduates, who do not look at the call centre industry as a long-term career, who are joining. Most of them see it as a transient job hop to greener pastures. The nature of work is better suited for women. Globally, over 70 per cent of the industry is powered by women, whereas in India less than 30 per cent of the employees are women. Women are more stable employees, though in developing countries still not the primary breadwinners. They do take a certain sense of pride in saying that they work for a big company like IBM, Accenture, or Wipro. Give women part-time jobs, give them flexible work hours, give them an option to get higher education, or reimburse their fees—all this will go a long way in ensuring a stable workforce. At 100 per cent attrition you cannot build a company. The BPO industry has to get its attrition levels down to about 30–40 per cent.

Attrition remains the primary problem for the industry. One interesting analysis indicated that attrition below 45 per cent would eat away your profits. Attrition at 45–50 per cent ensures that you have the right mix of entry-level workers (or freshers). If you have too many employees with more than two years of experience in the company, you will have a problem of a different dimension. You cannot create so many TL roles and TL salaries are 40–50 per cent higher than those of associates.

The Indian Railways operate at an attrition rate of less than 15 per cent. They attract good talent and have examinations, which people need to pass. The same is true with any large government establishment. What does the Indian Railways have that a BPO organization does not? The job of a typist, teller, clerk, and the like over the years has been and continues to be monotonous and boring. Yet, we never heard of counselling and help for these people. Why then the sudden demand for doing things differently for BPO employees. Is it the fact that BPO employees on average are very young, or the taxing timing of work, or the mismatch between expectation and reality that causes such high rates of attrition?

The biggest reason for people leaving a BPO organization is 'lack of self-respect and dignity'. This could be the result of the following:

1. Excessive zeal to meet CSAT scores, which in many cases are linked to variable pay.
2. TL wants to be at the top of the stack ranking as he faces pressure from his manager.
3. The manager is only two or three years older, is not a trained manager, and has his own set of favourites.
4. People are not seen as long-term assets—the use-and-throw mentality is prevalent in the organization.

While most companies focus on attrition in the operation floor, the bigger challenge is attrition during training, which is double that of attrition at the operation level.

Milind Godbole (MG) an industry veteran and chief development officer (CDO) at MphasiS, an EDS company, had a very valid point regarding the high attrition in the initial phase of an agent's lifecycle in a BPO. He says that in a typical BPO, one trainer comes in for four weeks to teach a group of agents. This is akin to a village school where you have only one teacher. Most people joining BPO firms are not toppers. They probably have studied in colleges where they have attended less than 50 per cent of the classes, bunking the rest, and spending most of their time in the cafeteria or with friends. Given this background, coming to an industry where you cannot come late for training or bunk training without prior intimation makes a person squirm. Every minute of your time in office is tracked in a BPO firm.

The three–four weeks of product training are not geared towards helping students and the new recruit is not able to get coached on his weakness. There is a lurking fear of disciplinary action or failing a test and being asked to leave.

After training, when a person lands up to take calls, he is just not geared to handle the challenge. It is like being thrown into a war zone. Training on accent and communication does not help when you are suddenly faced with callers talking in different accents. When anxiety takes a toll on you, you do not remember accent and the strong mother tongue influence creeps in. It is very natural for a person to forget the voice and accent neutralization coaching when placed in a stressful situation.

Imagine the plight of an agent who is just not trained to comprehend the problems of a caller who is talking to him in an accent he has never heard before. The first time, unable to understand the customer, the agent ends up disconnecting the call and leaves behind an irate customer. Very soon he realizes that this is not his cup of tea. Out of fear he leaves within days, or gets fired for disconnecting a customer's call and in the process causing end-user dissatisfaction as well as non-compliance with the call handling procedures. Even putting this agent in a refresher programme does not help him to get out of the anxiety or fear of rejection.

People who manage to survive the first few months in a BPO hang on and go on to succeed. Many others keep hopping from one BPO to another just attending the training sessions.

MG and his team monitored a group of 37 people who kept jumping from Wipro to EXL to MphasiS to V Customer to Ventura and WNS during a two-year period. They used to attend the training programme for three months and then leave to join the next company.

While it is good to have focus on metrics and attrition, it is equally important to be a sensitive and caring employer. This comes from company values. But sometimes, in the mad rush for growth, the fundamentals values are forgotten. Yes, most companies have value statements written on boards, but true implementation is a long way away.

Across the world, Indian BPO firms have the toughest performance management standards and this adds to the pressure.

Globally, it has been observed that call centres in countries that have union coverage have significantly lower rates of churn. There is predictability and the tendency to earn extra profit by running an operation on the borderline of a sweatshop is avoided. In the Philippines it is mandatory to pay the 13th month salary (or bonus) to entry-level BPO employees. A recent ruling in India stipulates that for people paid below Rs 10,000 per month, a 8.33 per cent bonus is compulsory and this has to be paid on a pro rata basis. This is a move in line with the Philippines mandate.

Sandeep, the managing director (MD) of Sapient India, was one of the earliest entrants into the Indian BPO industry. After completing his MBA, he worked for a few technology companies before joining Citibank in 1991. That was when Citi was setting up its back office centre. Sandeep and a team of four were amongst the first group of Indians to take calls at night. Since then Sandeep grew rapidly to become the president of MphasiS and is now MD at Sapient India. Having seen the growth and evolution of the industry very closely, Sandeep had some very interesting observations on the root cause of attrition.

According to Sandeep, if you look around, most of the professionals who run BPO companies and call centres come from a banking/finance profession, a fact which was whetted out while glancing through the speakers' profiles in the National Association of Software and Services Companies (NASSCOM) conference guide. Many of these CEOs started and sold off their company in a short span. Is this a reflection of our entrepreneurial spirit, but lack of long-term staying power?

In the initial days, start-ups gave customers the sun and moon to pick up orders. Initial contracts used to have utilization pegged at 85 per cent and annual productivity gains of 10–15 per cent were thrown in to sweeten the contract. The conditions on adherence and the average handling time (AHT) were equally attractive, probably much better than what the customer had in his own captive centre. And finally the price at US$ 10–12 an hour was unheard of globally.

All this resulted in business starting off by setting itself extremely tough deadlines to meet. An 85 per cent utilization to a layman looks achievable, but what this means is that a person needs to be on the phone for 51 out of 60 minutes in a hour and to do that for 8 hours, that is, the person needs to be on the phone 408 minutes out of 480 minutes. This is not humanly possible.

When you are on a call, you are using most of your senses—hearing, seeing the screen, typing on the keyboard, and your mind is working hard trying to resolve the issue—you really have to concentrate. Sandeep says it is impossible for a person to concentrate like this and achieve time utilization greater than 60–65 per cent.

Who set this 85 per cent utilization norm and why is it being followed over the years? Many attrition control meetings have taken place for discussing this.

The clauses that were part of contracts in the early part of the 2000s have stayed on, or most customers have tried to improve on them.

Why did the industry set itself these service level agreements (SLAs) and targets that are now boomeranging and becoming the challenge to be overcome.

Sandeep adds that this business is a sticky business. Most companies lack the guts to go and ask for higher rates or better terms. India has one of the lowest rates and the toughest SLAs. The person who signs the contract has no idea of how to run the business and uses past contracts as his reference. Customers always want to better their earlier contracts.

It is finally a choice that the management needs to make. If you have low rates, tough SLAs, and are keen to make high profits, then you will have high attrition rates and low salaries to pay.

To ease the attrition, companies need to ease the SLAs. If they ease the SLAs and still need to make the same profit margin, then they need to ask for higher rates.

Attrition in captives is lower not just because the pay is higher and they have better infrastructure, it is also because the SLAs are a lot less strict. If Indian companies are amongst the top three in CSAT scores, it is time that they asked for top rates also. This is the need of the hour. This will help the BPO industry get out of the catch-22 attrition problem.

Seven Steps to Control Attrition

Getting attrition under control would require seven steps to be followed diligently (see Figure 3.4).

It all starts with a strong hiring process that scouts for good talent and hires the right set of people. If you pay peanuts you get monkeys. You need to pay the right salary for the right talent to ensure market competitiveness.

The second step is to invest in training, not just for the new recruits, but for the TL and other people in the organization. Programmes need to be customized and need to deliver value.

The third step is to have a compensation structure that rewards performance and motivates stretch goals. The payouts need to be transparent and fair.

Career advancement and identifying the right roles for individuals is important. The key is customization and to create the environment of making employees feel wanted.

The fifth important step is to make things simple. Ensuring that the workload is equally distributed, agents and TL are not overloaded, and that there are not too many unwanted layers in the organization are important measures that need to be taken.

The sixth step is to choose a site which is not too crowded. Centres like Mumbai, National Capital Region (NCR), and Bangalore are poaching grounds for every new BPO organization that gets set up.

Figure 3.4: Seven Steps to Retention

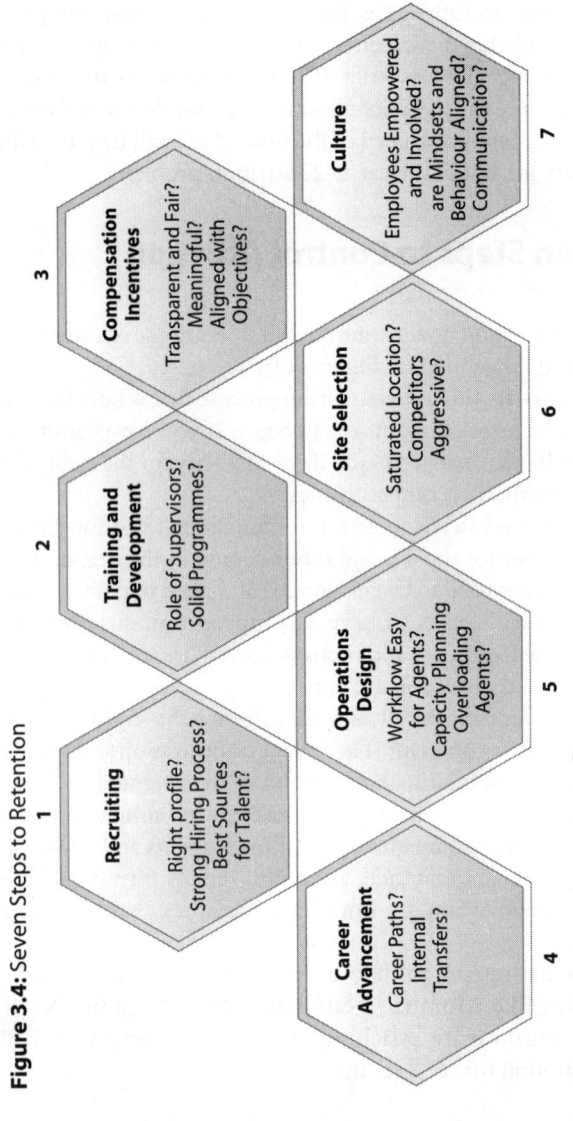

1 Recruiting
Right profile? Strong Hiring Process? Best Sources for Talent?

2 Training and Development
Role of Supervisors? Solid Programmes?

3 Compensation Incentives
Transparent and Fair? Meaningful? Aligned with Objectives?

4 Career Advancement
Career Paths? Internal Transfers?

5 Operations Design
Workflow Easy for Agents? Capacity Planning Overloading Agents?

6 Site Selection
Saturated Location? Competitors Aggressive?

7 Culture
Employees Empowered and Involved? are Mindsets and Behaviour Aligned? Communication?

Source: McKinsey Call Centre Practise Research.

And, finally, the last and most important step is to create a culture which is inclusive. Where communication flows, there is transparency and the leadership works in tandem with all employees towards achieving the company's goals.

These seven simple steps may sound easy to implement, yet no BPO company in India has been able to get its act together and implement these steps successfully.

Cost of Attrition

Attrition is like rust. A few of the larger companies hire 2,000 people per month and lose 1,500 in the first 90 days. The net addition is about 500 people. Trying to meet ramp plans and growth of 40 per cent with this level of attrition is impossible.

Not only does attrition hamper the growth of business, it also creates an organization with no values. Culture building is impossible and that again is one of the reasons why there is such high attrition. It is a vicious circle and the biggest problem in this industry.

Let us take an example of a company with 15,000 people and an attrition of 100 per cent.

The calculation given here will show that the cost of attrition equals the profit of the company. Data for this calculation was obtained after talking to five of the leading BPO companies in the country (see Table 3.1).

The cost of attrition has been worked out in detail after considering the following elements: salary, transportation costs, cost of training, cost of replacement (hiring cost), and other overheads.

The top reasons for attrition are:

1. Parity—my friend earns a higher salary.
2. Night shift job is against nature, it affects your health.

Table 3.1: Cost of Attrition Equals Annual Profits

Number of associates	15,000
Attrition rate/year	100%
Quarterly attrition	3,750
Attrition pattern	
Operations - 50%	1,875
First 30 days - 25%	937.5
First 60 days - 25%	937.5
Cost of Attrition/Person	
Cost of attrition in training (First 30 days)	Rs 35,000
Cost of attrition in training (First 60 days)	Rs 65,000
Cost of attrition in operations for tenured agent	Rs 85,000
Total Cost of Attrition	
Cost of attrition in training (First 30 days)	Rs 32,812,500
Cost of attrition in training (First 60 days)	Rs 60,937,500
Cost of attrition in operations for tenured agent	Rs 159,375,000
Total cost of attrition/quarter	Rs 253,125,000
Total cost of attrition/year	Rs 1,012,500,000
Total cost of attrition/year	US$ 24,700,000
Company with 15,000 associates would have revenues of	US$ 200,000,000
Profit at 12.5% of revenues	US$ 25,000,000

Source: Based on research conducted by the authors.

3. Military style of discipline, there is no time for a relaxed dinner.
4. Long commute time, try travelling in a packed seven-seater van in Delhi's summer with the temperature touching 45 degrees.
5. Lack of transparency in calculating leaves, variable pay, etc.
6. Preferential treatment by manager.
7. 9.5 hour job and 8.5 hours of calling time.
8. Stack ranking. Nobody likes to be at the bottom of the stack and have his name on the notice board.
9. Higher studies.
10. Peer pressure like a colleague joining a company at a higher salary.
11. Family pressure, lack of time with family.
12. Security concerns.

Key Measurement Parameters

The BPO business is a highly metrics driven one. In a well-managed BPO firm everything is measured and this is what drives the business to greater heights. Payments with most customers are transaction based and not based on time and material. When we checked across BPO companies we found that at a minimum there were over 200 parameters that were measured across operations and functions on a daily basis. Most BPO firms would have hundreds of people just collating MIS and preparing reports.

The top 12 business parameters used to run the business are listed in Table 3.2. This would be the tracker on which the CEO would have his eyes glued. Most of them are interlinked and it requires the deftness of an artist to manage so many parameters and deliver on customers and employee expectations and achieve profit before income tax (PBIT) and growth.

Table 3.2: Operating Parameters

Parameter	Industry Best Practice
Operating margin (post tax)	18–23%
Utilization (production agents/total agents)	60–65%
Agents in training	15–20%
Non-billable support staff	8–10%
Seat utilization (since people work in shifts, the same seat can be used by two people working in shifts. The best case scenario of seat utilization in a 24 hour day would be three assuming three shifts of 8 hours each)	1.4–1.6
Hourly realization/full-time equivalent (FTE) (varies across processes)	US$ 12–20 per hour
Annualized attrition (varies according to industry and type of work. Of this, training attrition is much higher than production attrition)	40–120%
Training throughput wing to wing (comprising induction, pre-process, process and on the job training)	75%
Met to offer ratio	10%
Employee referral hiring	25%
Channel hiring (varies from city to city)	50–60%
Cost of hiring associate	Rs 8,000–10,000/ hire

Source: Research conducted by the authors.

Cost Structure in a BPO Organization

1. The cost towards employee salaries and other staff expenses is 40–45 per cent.

2. The cost of infrastructure, telecom bandwidth, information systems, etc., is 15–20 per cent.
3. Business development and marketing cost account for 5 per cent.

In developed countries, the labour costs could be as high as 65–80 per cent of total costs. Brazil, India, Poland, and the Philippines have emerged as countries with the lowest labour costs across the globe.

Unique Challenges of the BPO Business

Being a 24x7 real-time business, the call centre business has some unique challenges:

1. High level of infrastructure redundancy.
2. Need for secure drop and pick up facilities for all employees.
3. Need for special staff welfare funding for fun and motivational activities.
4. High cost of training and hiring.
5. High levels of attrition given the stress due to working the night shift, or what is called the graveyard shift.
6. The need for physical and data security.

The challenges in a non-voice BPO organization are very different. Most of the data sent across are in the form of scanned documents. There are many errors in interpreting the same. These errors could result in liability claims on the parent customer. Small changes in mailing address can result in reminders and notices being sent to the wrong person. This communication gap can result in default of payments.

The biggest challenge facing the Indian BPO industry is to deliver value and move up the value chain. India is the first choice for iron ore, but not many look at India for finished steel products. Can the BPO industry cross the bridge and offer value beyond mere labour arbitrage? The coming years will help answer this question.

Rewards and Recognition/Fun Calendar

BPO is a high-pressure job. Most payment terms with customers are based on successful completion of transactions in pre-defined time. This is referred to as pay/transaction versus the time and material (T&M) model used in the IT industry. High pressure, long hours, monotony of the job, night shifts, long commute hours—all adds to the pressure. In captives, it is a little better—during an eight-hour shift, an agent would be on calls for four–five hours, while in a third-party firm it can be as high as seven hours. On some occasions, if there is shortage of staff, companies make agents work well beyond the stipulated eight hours to avoid losing revenue. The duration of a call in a third-party firm is also longer than in captives.

Companies have tried different approaches to ease the tension. In many companies there are designated fun managers, whose job is to organize ongoing activities. Festivals are celebrated with gaiety and theme parties are common. Many companies hold quarterly, half-yearly, and annual bashes, the scale of which is extravagant.

There is a designated budget for rewards and recognition (R&R). This varies from Rs 100 (US$ 2.5) per person per month to Rs 500 (US$ 12.5) per person per month. While the amount may look small, if you scale this to a company of 20,000 people, the kitty is massive—Rs 250 (US$ 6.25) per person per month adds up to a budget of Rs 60 million (US$ 1.5 million) per annum for company with a strength of 20,000 employees. While 50 per cent of this is spent in big bang high-impact events, the balance is spent on team dinners, birthday gifts, and, in some cases, even dating allowance.

Is Life a Marathon or a Sprint?

Do you get faster growth by changing jobs frequently or by sticking to the same one over a long period of time?

R&R—resign and re-negotiate—is a common practice across the industry. Even during the annual pay hike, one tends to see that the person, who has higher market value and is likely to threaten to resign, gets a better pay cheque. Loyalty is valued, but increasingly the feeling of loyal employees is that 'we are being taken for granted'.

People who job hop for salary increase get addicted to it. It is normal to see people switching jobs every one or two years at the middle and senior levels in the BPO industry. At the entry level, it happens every six months. The offer to join ratio at the middle and senior levels is 50–60 per cent since most people keep evaluating multiple offers at any point in time (see Figure 3.5).

Is this happening because organizations are not investing in building culture? Is there a difference between Company A and Company B?

It is easy to measure your job and benchmark yourself against the following parameters. Give yourself 10 if you are thrilled with any of these parameters and 0 if you are absolutely dejected. If you score below 30, it is time to look out for a new job. But before joining the company, ask your friends about the company and benchmark the new company also. There is no point in jumping from the frying pan into the fire.

1. Am I learning in my new job?
2. Do I see a clear growth path?

Figure 3.5: Options Galore

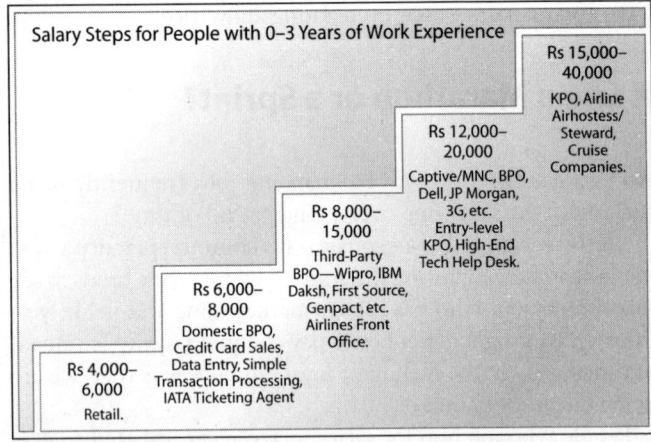

Salary Steps for People with 0–3 Years of Work Experience

Rs 4,000–6,000
Retail.

Rs 6,000–8,000
Domestic BPO, Credit Card Sales, Data Entry, Simple Transaction Processing, IATA Ticketing Agent

Rs 8,000–15,000
Third-Party BPO—Wipro, IBM Daksh, First Source, Genpact, etc. Airlines Front Office.

Rs 12,000–20,000
Captive/MNC, BPO, Dell, JP Morgan, 3G, etc. Entry-level KPO, High-End Tech Help Desk.

Rs 15,000–40,000
KPO, Airline Airhostess/Steward, Cruise Companies.

Source: Based on research conducted by the authors.

3. Is this a fast growing industry?
4. Is the environment of peers and managers positive?
5. Is my salary competitive?
6. Does the company I work for, treat me as an individual?

We asked over 50 people from various levels in five different companies to answer these questions and found that 80 per cent scored less than 30. The sad truth is that the grass on the other side is not as green as you perceive it to be.

We also plotted the career growth curve under three different scenarios over a 15-year period.

Scenario 1: A good performer stays in the same company for 15 years, is well taken care of, gets his promotion every two years, and sees a hike in his salary every year. The company trains him and rotates his job every three–four years.

Scenario 2: The same person decides to change jobs every six months for the first few years and then moves to a mode where he changes job every two years.

Scenario 3: The same person changes two jobs at strategic points in his career.

Our analysis is that the person in Scenario 3 is the most well rounded. He has the perspective of three companies, has invested time in learning and been smart enough to move when he felt he was hitting a glass ceiling because of lack of opportunities to grow.

While attrition on the operation floor is high because of various reasons, it is difficult to understand the high levels of attrition during training. Across the industry, the throughput in the first 90 days of training after a person joins varies from 45–75 per cent.

The worst case scenario of 45 per cent throughput means that if you hire 1,000 people a month and put them into a training programme, only 450 will be moving on to the operations floor to take calls. Of this 90 per cent will leave voluntarily, that is, they will abscond or leave without citing any reason. This is a dangerous trend and there is a sinking feeling amongst companies that there is a group of people who keep moving from company to company only attending training programmes.

Tougher joining norms and multiple rounds of screening have all not been able to get this number down significantly.

The answer to this is right-selling the job. Companies have come to realize that there is no point in spinning a web and selling a dream job by hiding the stark reality. Some of the advertisements for entry-level jobs have headlines like 'You deserve to be on the top', 'Get set to be the CEO', 'Are you ready to climb Mount Everest', and many more like these are setting wrong expectations from day one and are an attempt to oversell the job. If you cover the name of the companies in the advertisements you will not be able to differentiate between two companies because the messaging is so similar.

The positioning of the BPO industry in the initial days was questionable. Advertisements in 2002 positioned the industry as a fun place where you could party and make some quick money. This was a fundamental mistake and it was only in late 2005–06 that companies realized the mistake and the need to position the industry as a career versus a stopgap temporary job. The more you look at it, the more lucid it gets. Many of the problems that the industry is now battling with are issues that have been created by the industry itself.

A well drafted no nonsense letter stating the facts will go a long way in attracting the right talent. This linked with tighter selection procedures will see the right talent getting selected.

According to Sai Babu, head of sourcing at Wipro BPO, 'It's better to hire 1,000 people and lose 100 rather than hire 2,000 and lose 1,100.' Clearly this is the only way forward and the only way to stay away from the bottomless bucket phenomena.

We compared the training infrastructure between IT and BPO companies. The investment made in training rooms, lab infrastructure, training content, and even quality of trainers was far superior in IT companies.

Is the industry investing in BPO companies or using it as a cash cow? Do companies see the call centre industry as a robust scalable industry, or is the future strategy clearly to move from voice to the non-voice sector? There are companies that have clearly stated that the voice business will not exceed 25 per cent of their revenues, while others who started as call centre companies have in their five-year plan chalked out that the future business mix will be 75 per cent non-voice business and 25 per cent voice business.

Attrition in the voice business is high across the globe. If we look at the various rates in India, there is a lot of scope for Indian third-party companies to reduce attrition:

1. Indian third-party players have the highest attrition rates—50–100 per cent.
2. Well managed leading third-party players have attrition rates of 40–50 per cent.
3. Smaller captives have attrition rates of 30–40 per cent.
4. Attrition rates in third-party non-voice companies are at 25–35 per cent.
5. Non-voice captives have attrition rates of 15–20 per cent.

International call centres in developed countries like the US, Singapore, and Australia have attrition varying from 20–30 per cent, which compares with the best captive firms in India.

Why is attrition in Indian third-party BPO firms so high? If you look at parallels in companies in the high-pressure service industry like Café Coffee Day, McDonalds, and Pizza Hut— they all pay lower salaries, but have a lower attrition rate. Retail chains and companies like FedEx have high attrition rates, but there is pride in the job. The largest employer in India is the Indian Railways. Even they have attrition less than 15 per cent. Why is it that the Indian Railways has attrition less than 15 per cent while BPO companies have 80–90 per cent attrition?

The TLs can play a crucial role in reducing attrition. They are the first line of managerial control and have the highest level of engagement with agents. Ravi Venkatesh of OnTrack has developed a customized training programme for TLs, which not only helps them to manage their group on operating parameters, but also to help reduce attrition. Ravi propagates the concept of a value basket. He says that TLs should be trained to build a value basket for their team members. Given a choice if agents can choose between their TLs, who would they choose? What differentiates one TL from another?

In the value basket, the TL must perform a set of value-adding activities for each individual in her team. Whenever an agent thinks of leaving the company, the agent will then evaluate the new company against all of these value-adding activities, and not just look at the money being offered by the new company, before making the decision to quit. The TL programme run by OnTrack focuses on some of the following value-adding activities:

1. Success in current job: Everyone wants to be successful in his or her current job. However, not everyone knows how. Therefore, one item in the value basket will be the coaching-monitoring-feedback cycle that is intended to improve the performance of agents. This cycle is frequently underestimated. Not too many TLs are taught how to coach. Most of them end up telling agents what to do, rather than showing them how to do the job. For example, TLs may tell their agents that they need to reduce their handle time from 10 minutes to seven minutes within two weeks. They may even put them through an action plan. However, they do not teach their agents how to achieve this result. To show agent how to achieve results, TLs need to get down to the nitty-gritty. This involves analysis. For example, TLs may figure out that an agent has a high handle time because of certain types of calls. Within these types of calls, the agent has a high handle time because of inability to document properly at the end of the call. Therefore, a razor-sharp focus on after call work for specific types of calls could solve the problem. Such detailed work will enable agents to see that the TL is genuinely interested in their success. This is one reason why they would want to work only for their TL.

2. Focus on future career: Everyone has career aspirations beyond their current jobs. If agents see that their current job offers a path towards their future career aspirations, then they are likely

to stay longer in the company. Therefore, TLs have to play the role of career counsellors and need to perform career-planning activities. They need to create succession plans for every one of their team members. This plan will consist of names of agents, the next role they want to get into, and a target date by which the TL and the agent will finish preparing the agent for that new role. The goal is to ensure that the agent has the best shot at making it through an internal job posting (IJP) after preparation. If the agent qualifies for the IJP, the TL should spend time preparing the agent by administering mock tests, mock interviews, etc. TLs can also focus on agents who have other long-term career objectives, for example, some may want to do an MBA while others may want to become software engineers, etc. Even in these situations, the TL can help team members. Every additional month that agents stay with the company increases the average tenure of people.

3. Training: Training is a great way to increase competencies and capabilities of agents. While most TLs focus on process-related training (which they must do anyway), they do not realize that developing agents on other parameters will add value to an agent's capabilities. For example, TLs can train agents on new skills (for example, use of Word, Excel, PowerPoint, etc.). They can choose to train agents on a variety of other topics including time management, importance of personal savings, career opportunities in various departments, changing attitudes, how to get jobs done in various departments, aspects of the TL's own job, etc. The list is infinite. Each training session need not be longer than 10 minutes and it should not take more than 15 minutes to prepare the programme itself. Every month, the TL must conduct three–five such sessions. If this happens, the agent observes that he is getting smarter by staying with this TL.

4. Extra responsibility: Giving extra responsibility to agents is another way to get them engaged with the team/company. For instance, many companies have the concept of single point of contact (SPOC). An agent can be made a SPOC for a certain activity, for example, transportation, customer complaints, training, etc. But the way an agent is made a SPOC is where the

problem lies. Giving the title of a transport SPOC to an agent may make him feel good for a few days, after which he realizes that there is nothing much to do in the job, or that the job does not have much value. On the other hand, if the TL spends time and teaches the agent all the tasks involved, how to collect data on these tasks, how to analyse the data, how to draw charts and trend lines, how to do top problem analysis, etc., the agent feels that the job of the SPOC is important. The agent also learns all the skills that will help him move to his next role.

5. Delegation: Many TLs and managers feel that they are the only people who can do a particular task or job. Therefore, they do not delegate their jobs as much as they should. Delegation is a great way to develop competencies in an agent. The agent also feels motivated for having been given an important task. However, the moment a job is delegated, TLs must understand that there will be a performance problem. The agent will not be able to do the job as well as the TL. For this drop in performance, the TL must be ready to take the heat from his manager. He must also be ready to compensate for this drop in performance by putting in extra hours to coach the agent. At this point, if the TL decides to take back the job and do it himself, then he will be back to square one. However, consistent coaching, monitoring, and feedback will enable the agent to improve upon the job and over a period, the agent may do the job better than the TL.

6. Focus on family: A key element of Indian culture is family involvement in any major decision that any member of the family makes. For example, if an agent decides to change jobs, the family will most likely be involved. Therefore, if the TL takes the effort to establish closer ties with the agent's family, he can add an extra layer of friction that will discourage the agent from quitting. For instance, if an agent does something significantly good at work, the TL can call up his parents. He can introduce himself and then talk about the good job that the agent has done. When the agent gets back home, he will get a pleasant surprise because his parents will tell him about how happy his boss (the TL) is. If the agent ever thinks of quitting

his parents will most certainly ask questions to check if the agent is making the right decision.

7. Standing up for the team: TLs are closest to their team members. While they need to ensure smooth functioning of their teams by implementing management decision, they also need to educate their managers about the realities on the ground. For instance, if the workload is high, and agents are expected to put in more hours/days, the TL will communicate this to his agents. However, if there is an agent who is already overworked or is stressed, the TL must inform the manager that further stress will push the agent to quit the company, which is worse than him not working the extra hours. When agents see the TL standing up for them, they will have one more reason to stay in the team.

8. Setting expectations about career growth: TL and agents need to understand the value of staying in one company for a significant period of time. At a time when jobs are aplenty, agents tend to look at their careers in one-year blocks rather than five-year blocks. It is very tempting to jump jobs for more money. However, such jumps will only slow down a person's career in the long run. In the short run, the jump will fetch more money, but in the long term, the agent loses out because his colleagues who did not jump will have the benefit of tenure, and therefore increased competencies. Agents who change jobs frequently need to restart themselves in the new jobs time and again.

TLs need to set expectations with their agents and themselves that career growth is like the chart of the stock market. While it has its ups and downs, the long-term trend is always up. Therefore, when an agent quits a company because he is facing some problem, it is like looking at a short period of the stock market during which it was down and therefore getting out of the market.

TLs need to tell agents that if they learn to handle tough situations, it prepares them for bigger things in life. Tough situations can be professional or personal. Professional issues could be a bad boss, lower than market salaries, problems with colleagues or clients, loss of promotions, etc. Personal issues could be longer travel time, marriage, money problems, and relationships.

TLs also need to tell agents that there are some people who have been very successful by constantly changing jobs. However, such people are very few in number and their success is like winning a lottery ticket. One does not plan one's career around a lottery ticket. Therefore, the only long-term sustainable strategy is to develop oneself by staying in a company for a significant period.

9. Becoming interesting: The TL must become an interesting person to work with. As the saying goes, 'All work and no play makes Jack a dull boy.' If the only thing agents hear from their TL are work-related issues, the TL may be perceived to be a 'boring' person. Instead, the TL must make an effort to discuss various issues with agents. TLs can develop such qualities by reading books on a variety of subjects, reading newspapers, etc. It would be a pleasant surprise for the agents if their TL discussed the future of space travel with them, or the results of the recent by-elections, the latest medical advances, the latest book by Dan Brown, etc.

10. Creating a motivating environment: This has become a cliché in BPO circles. However, TLs who are able to create a motivating environment are likely to keep their team members together for a longer period of time. Motivation does not necessarily have to come through fun events such as pizza parties, celebrations, team outings, etc. They can also come through serious events like arranging a talk by the VP of quality on career opportunities in the field of quality or a mock test/quiz to allow agents to test themselves to see if they are ready to become TLs, quality analysts, trainers, etc. TLs must maintain and publish a monthly 'events calendar' where they need to plan for motivational events for the entire month. Agents will look forward to these events and are likely to remain more engaged.

These items in the value basket are just a sample of a vast number of items that the basket can actually contain. Every TL must build the value basket based on his or her strengths.

Developing TLs to create these value baskets can be the strategic weapon companies are looking for to combat attrition. TLs are the critical layer who can help in changing the perception among agents that BPO jobs are just another commodity.

We spoke to Ashok Agrawal, director of Kaleidoscope Events, a leading event management company servicing corporate accounts and working actively with many BPO firms. He has had no attrition in his company in the last two years. Ashok has a core team of 26 people across the country and says that the workload in an event management company is sheer murder and the salaries are nothing to write home about. The reason for low attrition in his company according to him are basically because of the following:

1. There is clear job definition and no overlap of functions.
2. There are limited layers. There are only three layers including himself.
3. There is high focus on reward and recognition for teams.
4. There is personal connect and touch time with all employees.
5. There are well defined rules and the management plays by those rules.

Ashok feels that the challenge in the BPO industry is lack of discipline. While there is a similarity with the manufacturing industry, a worker on the shop floor does not have the options that the BPO employee has.

BPO employees belong to a generation that does not like rules—they have had multiple choices from the time they were born. The minute you hurt the dignity and self-respect of the people of this generation, they are bound to leave, which is probably the reason the attrition rate is so high, says Ashok.

We can now extrapolate this to the lower attrition rates in places like McDonalds and Pizza Hut where there is a very well defined job role and the sense of team spirit is very high. A high school student comes punctually at 5 a.m. in the morning to sweep the unit where he is working because that discipline is ingrained in him during his training period. This culture is very similar to military discipline, where people take pride and joy in doing even menial work.

Shombit Sengupta, a global growth strategy consultant, has also spent time analysing the youth trend. Shombit sees the current generation, with its radical thought processes and behavioural traits, to be the torchbearers of change, the most important ingredient in India's future as a global business leader. Shombit calls them the ZAP86 generation and categorically confirms that they influence the overall purchase decision in every home today.

Why ZAP86? Because, the tendency of those born in and after 1986 is to experiment with everything that is new, flit from subject to subject, like zapping television channels. Babies born in 1986 became five-years-old in 1991, when economic reforms were introduced in India. At the age of five, a child can consciously start making decisions. People from this generation onwards have thrived in a booming, liberalized economy. Their upbringing, attitude, and values are very different from Indians of yesteryears. As a result of 100 years of British rule and a protected economy since Independence to 1991, the needs, habits, desires, and aspirations of the older generations had become very flat. Opening up the country to foreign players brought intense market competition resulting in consumers getting an enormous choice for the first time in the Indian market. Those born after 1986 are exposed to society's new character, and so they sport very divergent world views and attitudinal approaches.

Shombit believes that the ZAP86ers have an individual spirit with a dash of self-indulgence. Except for non-aggression, they are not ready to carry the older values of sacrifice, savings, being dominated by elders, or being submissive in any sense. The earlier generation lived for their parents and their children; the ZAP86 generation, having grown up in an atmosphere o choice, live for themselves. They are not seeking the security of a steady job, they do not suppress thoughts on sex and nor are they in any compromising mode. In a nutshell, these are the traits ZAP86ers have:

1. Speed of technology: They want to discover and have no time to stand and stare.
2. Code language: Their communication is crisp and digital; they have fun networking.
3. Egotism: Self is more important than others.
4. Global thought and knowledge: They are responsible and are concerned about global issues like global warming. They also prefer global entertainment.
5. Sexual liberation: They like to live independently without any restrictions and believe that expression of feelings should not be curbed.
6. Flirtation with jobs: They are career-oriented. They prefer private jobs as they are merit-oriented unlike government jobs that are seniority dependent.
7. Self-indulgence: They believe in a culture of spending rather than saving. Live for today and do not carry any baggage of yesterday is their motto.
8. No role models: They want to create their own role models and have an inclination towards entrepreneurship.

Shombit is of the view that professionals in the age group of 45+ years who run business organizations in India are totally disconnected from the ZAP86 generation in spite of having children in that age group. To sustain business tomorrow, he says, the industry has to make the effort to understand the ZAP86 generation in depth, and any process or value creation of every deliverable has to be based on this generation.

There are multiple factors that pressurize a BPO agent and the biggest hassle is that of an invisible customer and a military style of management. The combination of this makes it a very stressful job (see Figure 3.6).

Figure 3.6: Multiple Pressure Points in the Life of an Agent

Source: Research output from Shining Strategic Design.

128

Building Culture and Value

How do you build culture and value system in a company when the churn is so high? It is an arduous task when generation-next is working with the clear intent of a short-term job and not a career. Globally one-third of the employees in a call centre are part-time or temporary staff. Most of them are sourced through a third-party temping company.

Do executives in BPO companies see human capital as the core of it's organization? Are they investing in people for the long term? Are they building a company on values?

It boils down to certain basics. Many companies shy away from the need to invest in people, thinking they are not going to stick around for long. They question the time, effort, and money spent on developing and training people.

It is a question of taking the initial initiative. If you do not make an effort, things will deteriorate further. But the question here is who takes the first step? It has to be the employer. Progress will be slow, but it will have an impact and that is when leaders will stand out from the rest.

The gauntlet needs to be picked up by companies who want to stand above the crowd. As Gandhiji said, 'Find purpose and the means will follow.'

Successful leaders in the BPO industry would need the qualities listed in Table 3.3.

Table 3.3: Attributes of Successful Leaders in BPO Organizations

Attribute	%
HR/People skills	25
Finance skills	20
Metrics and quality	25
Technology and systems	10
Sales	20

The behavioural competencies of leaders at a BPO company would include the following qualities as listed in Table 3.4.

Table 3.4: Behavioural Competencies of Successful Leaders in BPO Organizations

Competence	%
Execution	50
Conceptual thinking, strategy, creativity, innovation	25
Service orientation, customer satisfaction, people skills, empathy	25

If you have these qualities, then the BPO industry will welcome you with open arms.

What Drives Structured Chaos?

Every industry that has grown has had some captive source, which acted as a foundation for growth. When the telecom industry in India started growing, a large part of its workforce was sourced from public sector companies like Bharat Sanchar Nigam Limited (BSNL) and Mahanagar Telephone Nigam Limited (MTNL). Many professionals and technologists from the US and Europe also joined up with the Indian telecom majors.

The private airlines industry in India has taken off thanks to people from Indian Airlines, Air India, and the Indian Air Force who joined these private players. They have also attracted talent from overseas.

Private hospitals like Apollo, Manipal, and Escorts have grown thanks to doctors joining them from government hospitals and US and UK returned doctors who joined them.

Private banks like HDFC, ICICI, Kotak, Yes Bank, Citibank, etc., were able to draw upon the strong foundation of the Indian public sector banks. So is the case of private sector insurance companies, which attracted talent from Life Insurance Corporation (LIC) as well as foreign collaborations.

Sadly, the BPO industry did not have any base to draw upon and it did not attract tenured veterans from international centres.

In the initial days, when you thought of a BPO company, you thought of customer service and this led to people from hotels, airlines, door-to-door sales representatives, etc., joining

BPO firms. Right from middle to senior management, most of the people running a BPO had never seen the true life on the floor. As the industry grew and attracted some bright talent, the problem still continued.

If you ask a smart MBA to reduce transportation cost, he will come up with a solution to do away with customized home pick up and drop facilities and will suggest a trunk pick up from a location. While this solution works well on paper, the reality is that no Indian parent will want his daughter to wait on the streets at 10 p.m. in the night. There is no option but to have customized pick up and drops from the alleys and lanes of our towns and cities.

Whether it is pricing or running an efficient transportation system, the challenge at a BPO is that the people who take these decisions higher up, do not have a complete picture of what happens at the grass-root levels. Pricing is done by sales and finance people who agree to conditions and SLAs that are not possible to deliver. The SLAs are not benchmarked with historic data or even with the performance at the captive's own centre.

Another question worth asking is why is there a resistance to increasing rates and having realistic performance targets? Getting a client engagement started and making it work successfully takes over six months. During this time, clients can drop on their CSAT scores and even lose customers. There is no guarantee that the new partner will deliver what the client demands, because clients will tend to squeeze out the same or lower rates from the new service provider.

However, the perception in the industry is that clients can change their outsourcing partner (that is, change the vendor) easily without incurring any high transfer cost.

It is a myth that the cost of changing partners is huge. No customer will want to change an engagement that is delivering high CSAT scores. Pricing needs to be linked to relative CSAT scores.

We spoke to the outsourcing team of a large US financial services company to obtain the views of the customer and some very interesting points came up.

Customers clearly look at outsourcing for cost reductions. In most cases, a target is given, which could be as high as 40–50 per cent savings.

In the initial stages of evaluation, customers look for the best deal—low cost, large stable partners with presence in multiple locations/countries.

Very soon the aspect of quality and standards come into the picture and now the demand is not only low cost, but also stringent adherence to global standards.

Large companies have a clear outsourcing strategy. Initially they start a pilot with a domestic partner and test out their process maturity. The second phase would be to partner with an offshore vendor. Companies have a clear strategy on the number of seats to be outsourced, number of suppliers to be had, and the number of cities and countries to which they will expand. This strategy is followed diligently.

In most cases, the business grows because of relationship and trust. Large companies with a centralized supply chain have a better control on day-to-day functioning. However, there are many instances of individual business units doing it on their own. Such relationships struggle after some time.

The biggest challenge for customers is the Indian mindset of not being able to proactively highlight challenges and issues. The middle management in Indian companies is not assertive and easily accepts all the pressure points from the customer. They are not proactive in communicating and hence do not raise the alarm when things start going wrong. Customers feel that if Indian managers are more open and increase their communication then the relationship can flourish better.

Company officials say that this is an Indian culture. Added to this is the sensitivity towards customers. Any complaint received from a customer against an individual is treated with the highest seriousness. Across companies, individuals against whom complaints have been received either get changed or in some cases their services are terminated. This is a subconscious fear in the mind of middle managers, which makes them very submissive.

In many companies, the CEO and top management agree to the tough conditions laid down by the customer and force the middle management to comply with these conditions. The middle managers are not able to stand up and resist such measures, and this often leads to souring of relationships. In many cases, the root cause of the problem is lack of consistency of information between the layers of the company. In many organizations, the middle management is not involved in, or does not have knowledge about the nitty-gritty of contracts. Many have not even seen the SLAs or the contract.

A leading service provider did a Six Sigma project on contract standardization. At the end of six months they had to disband the team because the information was scattered and fragmented. Many commitments on important contract changes are on email, which never get translated to annexures and amendment terms in the contract. In many cases, people who made commitments on email had left the company and nobody had a clue about what was committed.

The other challenge of customers is over dependency on a few individuals. Across organization, relationships are built based on the comfort with a few individuals. The challenge comes in when there is a change of people. Customers begin to question the robustness of the company's process.

So, how do you run a healthy relationship where both the customer and the partner can benefit mutually? In many relationships, it becomes one-sided. The demand from the customer is stringent, cooperation and help in areas like training and attrition control is minimal. These one-sided demands over a period of time are detrimental to the relationship and a point comes when the partner says enough is enough.

The approach of standing up and telling a customer, 'Thank you, I cannot serve you at these conditions' was first started by Infosys. In the late 1990s, during the dot-com boom, Infosys made history in the outsourcing industry by standing up to General Electric (GE) and refusing business against low rates and very stringent terms and conditions. This trend was followed by a few other companies. In the recent past, we have seen signs of this in the BPO industry, where company executives have decided to walk away from business rather than accept detrimental conditions that are entirely one-sided. This is an indication of a positive trend, which will help companies in the long run.

The challenges of captives are very different from those of third-party players. Locals working in a captive are never clear of what the intent of the parents is. Is there more work coming, do we get ready for scale, are we going to be sold—these are some perpetual questions at the back of the mind of employees in a captive firm. There is always an invisible force taking decisions. The cost of operations, needless to say, is 30–40 per cent higher than third-party firms. Since the payment is not linked to SLAs, the performance in captives with better paid executives tends to be lower.

Given the size and stature of the industry, it is time the industry stood up and started claiming its dues. We would like to suggest the following:

1. If you have global centres, offer the customer one blended rate. Measure on delivery and performance. It is time the industry stood up and told customers not to micromanage their operations.

2. Contract SLAs need to be benchmarked with client's performance at his own captive centres. Contract terms should offer bonus for achieving more. Currently, contracts have more penalty and less reward.

3. Performance improvement is a joint responsibility.

4. Most contracts cover the cost of associates or agents. Like the IT industry, the cost of every person associated with operations right till the AVP dedicated to the account needs to be considered. The current pricing of US$ 12–14 an hour for an associatet covers overheads of all layers in operations and support functions. Pricing is always based on entry-level salary and does not take tenure into consideration. The IT industry even charges for bench. In many cases, the same customer who agrees to pay for IT acts tough for the BPO contract.

5. The current span of control is 12–18 per TL/unit load. This has to be reduced to 5.

6. Contracts need to be signed in local currency to avoid fluctuations.

7. Rate increases need to keep in touch with real inflation. A 4–5 per cent rate increase annually does not cover even the cost of inflation.

Companies also need to ensure that controls are set in at the right place. Many companies start hiring and training people even when the final negotiations are going on. The greed for rapid growth results in many BPO firms setting up infrastructure and having 1,000–2,000 seats ready. This is counter productive in many cases, as firms end up offering the customer a killer deal just to fill up their open capacity.

What bothers industry veterans is that today's leaders lack the courage to call a spade a spade. Every CEO is smart enough to know what needs to be done. But the incessant demand for growth and profitability limits them. Most leaders are hesitant to change a model that is delivering profits. So complex is the cycle of events and interconnections that CEOs are scared to make any change because they are not sure what the impact will be. The fear to make changes arises from the fear of whether the profits the CEO has struggled so hard to achieve will disappear after the change and whether attrition levels will stay the same after the change.

Where is the sense of unity amongst Indian businesses? Every business runs on the basis of mutual benefit. Is there any place in the world which can absorb the work of 600,000 people? In an earlier section we saw that the average salary of a call centre agent in India is 10 times lower than the global standard. As an industry can we not unite and set some norms? Can the industry not decide on a bare minimum rate/SLA norm? Do we need the leftists and the unions to come and create this model? Why are we defensive? When the union health minister of India makes a request to the industry to try and provide help to BPO employees with regard to their health, the first reaction was to protest. Why is there denial? Why can industry leaders not face the truth and work on improving in areas where there is a crying need for change?

Should we fall prey to this and choke a thriving energetic industry in its adolescence. It is time for the industry to think long term. It is time for the investors and leaders to change their trader mentality and look at this industry as a cash cow. It is time for the leaders to look at BPO as the rising star, which can continue to maintain its growth in a healthy manner taking all in its wake.

Let us remember the parable of the farmer who had a duck, which gave him a golden egg every day. One day out of impatience and greed, he throttled the duck to collect all the golden eggs it had inside. The farmer lost out in the long term. Let us hope that the BPO industry does not follow this route.

CHAPTER 4

Working in a BPO

The Indian youth need to mouth a silent prayer of thanks to BPOs for creating an opportunity to get started with their careers. Not just work, but decent work that earns a handsome starting salary. If not for the BPOs most of the 600,000 people employed in the Indian BPO sector would be either unemployed or struggling at jobs paying far less. (India's per capita income is less than US$ 500 per annum while the average BPO employee's starting salary is US$ 250 per month.)

By definition a job is hard work. You are not paid to party, but to deliver consistently and follow the routine and discipline chartered by your employer. The initial years in any job across industries is tough—doctors slog for years as interns working 18-hour shifts; hotel staff work long hours at low salaries; nurses have highly demanding crucial jobs and are paid low wages; in the construction industry, civil engineers work long hours under tough conditions; fast moving consumer goods (FMCG) executives and medical representatives travel from shop to shop, clinic to clinic trying to meet their daily targets; the list can go on and on.

The BPO industry is an oasis compared to many other industries. Think of any other job where you have heard of amenities like home pick up and drop facilities, doctor at your office, a gym to workout at, counselling sessions available free of cost, subsidized food in cafeterias (many companies even provide free meals), library, yoga rooms, sports rooms, and a clean spacious air-conditioned office—all of this packaged in a casual, friendly, and cool college-like environment.

While on one side we hear of the challenges of working in a BPO firm, there are many who have stayed on and grown to senior positions, bonding closely with their peers, and developing a close fraternity that is as good as a family.

Aspirations versus Reality

The first step is setting realistic expectations. BPO companies are not waiting with banners saying 'Trespassers will be recruited.' The selection process is stringent and the work is hard—not everyone is suited to handle the pressures of a BPO. Once the expectation setting is right and you are able to hire the right talent, most of your problems are solved (see Figure 4.1).

Piyush Mehta, an industry veteran and the head of human resources (HR) at Genpact, is a strong believer in investing time and effort to hire the right talent. Genpact puts all potential hires through a programme that simulates work in a BPO firm. At the end of this programme, candidates are given a choice to decide if they want to continue or leave. Nearly 10 per cent drop out after getting a deep insight into the industry. Piyush feels it is better that they leave early else the company ends up investing time and money in training people who will leave after 30–60 days.

Figure 4.1: Aspiration versus Reality

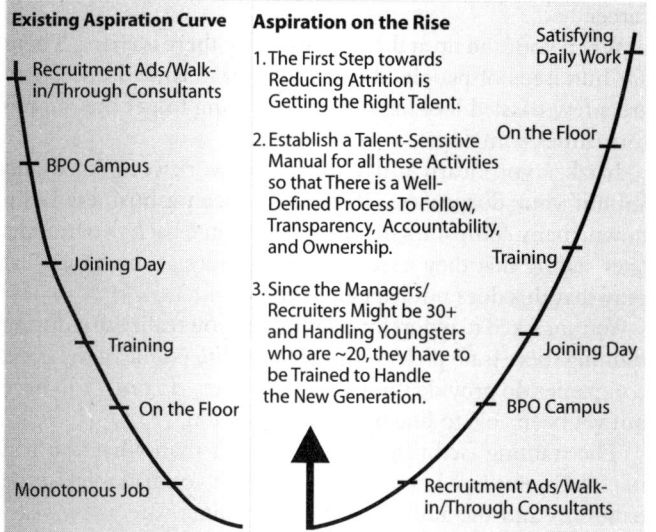

Existing Aspiration Curve

Recruitment Ads/Walk-in/Through Consultants

BPO Campus

Joining Day

Training

On the Floor

Monotonous Job

Aspiration on the Rise

1. The First Step towards Reducing Attrition is Getting the Right Talent.

2. Establish a Talent-Sensitive Manual for all these Activities so that There is a Well-Defined Process To Follow, Transparency, Accountability, and Ownership.

3. Since the Managers/Recruiters Might be 30+ and Handling Youngsters who are ~20, they have to be Trained to Handle the New Generation.

Satisfying Daily Work

On the Floor

Training

Joining Day

BPO Campus

Recruitment Ads/Walk-in/Through Consultants

Source: Research output from Shining Strategic Design.

Imagine you are a 20-year-old, studying in a college in a small city like Jamshedpur. You have grown up reading great things about the IT-BPO boom. In your mind, companies like Wipro and Infosys are as great as Microsoft and IBM. You are in awe when you get to hear that a big marquee name is visiting your campus to recruit people. The posters, banners, and handouts all spell one word—wow! Good salary, great benefits, career growth, the marketing spins a magic web. You are ready to give your left hand to join the job.

The interview process takes nearly a day and you wait for your turn. If you are good you get selected and have an offer the very same day, asking you to join when you have completed your examinations. During this time you get letters and calls at home reminding you not to forget the date with your dream career.

When you land up at the campus/office there is chaos. There are hundreds of people like you who have landed up. There are a few hassled looking office staff trying to get the joining formalities completed.

It takes you nearly a day to get the work completed and submit your documents. If there has been a business ramp down, many companies may ask you to come back two months later stating that they have no opportunities at this time. Just pray that this does not happen to you.

You are asked to report for training and you realize that during training there is no pick up and drop facility (some of the good companies do provide this facility, but many do not). You have not yet been able to line up accommodation.

The training facilities are okay—better than what you had in college, but nowhere in line with what you had seen in the handouts and the audio-visuals. The trainers are a few years older than you, many of them are not very courteous, and they are not very helpful. The rote training of school and college seems to be the model here also. In the midst of training, time flies as you try to arrange for accommodation and try to get acclimatized to the new city.

Young trainers have a sudden sense of power over the freshers, which in many cases translates into arrogance. In most companies, a batch is trained by just one trainer for the entire duration. In a school or a college, a professor can take classes for two–three hours. In a BPO company, trainers take classes continuously for eight hours. A sense of boredom and fatigue creeps into trainers also. The sense of power and control is what keeps them going in most cases.

The students in training are forced to maintain a military style of discipline, be punctual, not use their cell phones—practices which they have not adhered to in college. Being part of a varied group where the ages vary from 18–55 is also bewildering.

You see a lot of people suddenly missing from your training room. People not qualifying the tests are given a second chance, after which they are asked to leave. From a company perspective, this makes sense because they want to cut their losses and stop training for someone who they feel will not be able to meet the requirements on the operations floor.

However, for a fresher, getting his first job, this is a morale dampener. The last phase of training is on the job training (OJT). The OJT phase hits you hard—it is like moving to the war field from the training room. In most companies, only 80 per cent of freshers are able to get past the OJT phase. The best in class companies have a 90 per cent throughput.

Finally, you make it to taking calls on your own and within a very short time the pressure on performance builds up. You are monitored closely. Added to this, you are not convinced why your variable pay is less than your colleagues. The smart-looking boys and girls, who have a good rapport with their managers, seem to be getting the highest variable pays. When you go to your manager and complain about this, it is not received well and you are looked upon as a troublemaker.

Very soon you realize that troublemakers are not invited to the parties and also end up getting the worst shift duties. When you ask for leave, it is denied.

Team leaders (TLs) and people manning the command centre are extremely powerful. They control even your visits to the toilet. They are also the people who decide your leaves and shifts. They also decide the termination lists.

As you stay on through these challenges, you suddenly see that the people who are good at Excel and PowerPoint are getting promoted as TLs. Every manager gets his entire work of reporting and presentation done by TLs who are good at PowerPoint and Excel.

We will talk about this in detail in a later section. Let us now take a look at the effect of working odd hours in a BPO firm.

Effect of Odd Hour Work Schedule

Most call centres in India operate 24x7. They have customers in the United States (US), United Kingdom (UK), and Australia. The bulk of the staff operates for the US and UK clients and the working time across call centres can be split between the US and UK shifts (see Figure 4.2).

Figure 4.2: Time Schedules in a Call Centre

A Day in the Life of a BPO Worker
When India sleeps, the BPOs wake up to work. Here's how your workday would be if you worked in a BPO.

US 'PROCESS' **For a shift that starts at 10:30 p.m.**

RAMEN SARKAR

7 p.m. Get up and Get Ready, eat.
8 p.m. Pick-up Cab Arrives.
10 p.m. Reach Office
10:30 Log in
12:30 First Break for 15 Minutes
3:30-4 a.m. Breakfast Break
6 a.m. Can Take an Early Break or can Log-off Early
7 a.m. Board Cab

Source: 'BPO's Young and Troubled', *Business Today* (June 2007).

As operations take place 24x7, you need people on the floor at all times. Even when it is 12 midnight in the US and 12 in the afternoon here, you need a skeletal staff to take the odd calls that filter through.

This results in over 48 shift timings in a day, the worst shift, called the graveyard shift, starts at 1.30 a.m. just after midnight and ends at 10 a.m. in the morning. Employees leave home at 12 midnight and come back at 12 noon. It messes up your entire system. Before people settle down to certain shift timings, their routine changes again and this adds to further chaos.

Psychologists fear that the long hours of work will impact the health of BPO employees. Loss of identity, isolation, and stress force many employees to seek boosters and medication to keep going.

The combination of night shifts, long hours at a demanding job, and high stress eventually takes its toll on your health. In industry parlance this is called burn out stress syndrome (BOSS). The symptoms include chronic fatigue, insomnia, eye strain, weight loss, severe acne, and complete alteration of the 24-hour biological rhythm of the body. Gastrointestinal problems are inevitable, sleep disorders are common, and women may face severe gynecological problems. Many of these do not surface immediately but appear later in life.

People working in BPO firms are from middle-class families. They do not have separate rooms. Many families live in small 600 sq. ft apartments. It is very difficult to try and get sleep at daytime in a small apartment where you live with a large family, especially in a densely populated and noisy neighbourhood.

Workplace stress is a hotly debated topic worldwide. It is estimated that workplace stress eats into profits worth US$ 300 billion annually. A lot of that is in the BPO industry.

There is a role that employees need to play to mitigate this stress. There are very clear indicators to know when your stress alarm is ringing:

1. Low morale.
2. Poor communication.
3. Increase in absenteeism.
4. Higher attrition.
5. Increase in customer complaints.
6. Rudeness/arguments among co-workers.
7. Phone rage.

All these are common symptoms that we see in the BPO workforce.

The impact of workplace stress is dangerous and can erupt in any of the following ways:

1. Mistakes/accidents.
2. Low morale.
3. Increase in alcoholism/ drug abuse.
4. Workplace violence/harassment.
5. Fudging of information.
6. Loss of productivity.

Again, these are clearly visible in the Indian BPO industry.

The cause for stress can be:

1. Uncontrollable: Economic/political.
2. Employer controlled: Culture, organizational structure, physical factors, environment, communication, management style, policies, procedures, workload, and schedules.
3. Employee controlled: Home, family, internal thinking, and perceptions.

While the external factors are difficult to change, the employer and employee-controlled factors can be addressed suitably to reduce stress. Counselling, proactive measures, and being a listening organization can go a long way in reducing workplace stress.

Many people from surrounding cities, working in BPO companies live in shared accommodation. Four or five people share a small 12 ft x 12 ft room. This is not a problem only for associates, but even for managers. You hardly get time with your family and this affects your work and home-life balance. Employees in BPO firms have a very high marriage breakdown rate. There are many couples who meet only over the weekend— the wife works in a day shift job from 8 a.m. to 7 p.m. and the husband in a night shift job from 6 p.m. to 5 a.m.

A study by the Seattle-based Fred Hutchinson Cancer Institute indicated that women who work night shift might face an increased risk of breast cancer at a later stage in life.

Many parents informed us that their high-energy children had become zombies within months of joining the industry. The initial days were enjoyable, but very soon they became edgy and short tempered.

One such instance is that of a lady who had joined a BPO firm and left the industry within nine months to take up a relatively easier low paying day job with a retail company. This is what she had to say, 'The call centre wanted to take more and more work, made impossible commitments, and pushed the employees to their limit. If the attrition was high, the people attending calls were at times asked to work for 12 hours. Getting a 15-minute lunch break was also a challenge. Rosters were made on a weekly basis. We could finish work at 3 p.m. on a Saturday and be asked to report at 7 p.m. the same day on the new roster. If you missed a day you lost your salary and if you asked for leave it was denied.'

She added, 'All this soon takes a toll. In less than six months from joining you are on the lookout. You have learnt how this industry operates. And you want to move to a place where the grass is greener. Your friend tells you to leave the day you get your pay cheque. He says just quit because if you go and inform your managers they will hold back your arrears.'

Another young BPO employee, who had spent over three years in three different BPO companies in Gurgaon said, 'While we are inside the company, we say BPO rocks, but when we are sitting in a pub with friends sharing our challenges, we say BPO sucks.'

Over 75 per cent of the people leaving BPO companies, leave without informing. The industry does not insist on a relieving letter and this works well for the employees. Every company reports their highest attrition rate during the first week of the month.

A large BPO company conducted a survey to capture the challenges faced by BPO employees in India ('BPO's Young and Troubled', *Business Today*, July 2007). The problems can be summarized as:

1. Odd work timings: Working at night and sleeping during the day upsets a person's natural bio-rhythm.
2. Monotonous job: Repetitive job that offers little diversity results in low job satisfaction.
3. Split personality: Assuming a different name while dealing with a foreign customer and putting up with his abusive tone and language leads to stress.
4. Performance targets: Close monitoring by supervisors and linkage of performance to pay leads to stress.
5. Cultural clash: Many BPO employees (nearly 25 per cent) come from small towns and have a tough time settling down in the large metros.
6. Low self-esteem: Comments like 'if he works in a BPO he must not have got a job anywhere else' affects a person's self-esteem.

These challenges are very specific to the call centre industry. The non-voice BPO firms do not have many of the challenges associated with the call centre business. Work here is similar to clerical work in a bank. The monotony level is high, but that is something people learn to live with.

Generation of Choice

The current generation has choice. For every 100 people, the selection ratio is at best 10. In second-tier and third-tier cities, it drops to as low as 3. For every advertisement and publicity exercise that is conducted, people come in hordes, but it is only a small percentage who pass the bar. Once they do, it is an entry to a world of rapid pay hikes. The working environment across BPO companies is not very different, however, there are companies that have invested time and effort to ensure excellent working conditions for their employees.

Sadly, many companies look at squeezing out their employees to the maximum possible. Work shifts of 10–11 hours against the stipulated eight (with no overtime pay), cars packed with five employees, very limited breaks, rare leaves, no emails, and hardly any knowledge of what is happening in the company are some of the other drawbacks.

Under these situations it is important that individuals take due diligence before joining companies. Larger established companies are trying their best to create a structure and resolve these problems. The HR departments are working overtime to ensure that employee rights are not jeopardized at any cost. When you plan to join a company or change jobs ask the following questions before taking a decision:

1. Have you understood your pay slip clearly? The figure at the bottom of your offer letter and what you receive at the end of the first month may vary a lot. Look for companies that give you clear documentation. Some companies are so transparent that they even have a section on frequently asked questions (FAQs) with the offer letters. Understand the fixed and variable components in your pay packet. Check your insurance limits. Check if provident fund (PF) is part of your package and do you have a permanent account number (PAN) number (equivalent to the social security number in the US) for your PF to be credited.

2. Talk to colleagues who work in the company and understand how good the company policies are. Are they just policies on paper or are they actually implemented? Is the voice of the employees heard?

3. If the company has both IT and BPO divisions, find out how easy it is to move to the IT division at a later date. Growth in career is critical. Determine the time and process taken for you to become a TL.

4. Does the company have part-time education programmes? Are there scholarships or funding for these programmes? Ask for a detailed list of the programmes.
5. Understand the attendance incentive programme and how it works.
6. Most companies have a night-shift allowance. Be clear on the timings for which the night-shift allowance is valid.

Piyush Mehta, head of HR at Genpact, rightly says, 'People still leave because of the following three reasons:

1. The way the organization and your boss treats you.
2. Career growth options.
3. Salary.

People do not leave because the cafeteria food was bad or the car did not pick you up on time.'

Good systems and practices will translate to lower attrition. The benefits of this cycle soon kick in—lower attrition saves you money and time, and the pressure on margins reduces.

Many companies are even investing in providing counselling for their employees. Says the head of HR at a large BPO organization, 80 per cent of the problems of the associates are personal. If we can help solve their personal problems they will be happy and will deliver at work. This is an indication of the effort that good companies are putting in to try and help the youth.

There have been instances of employees getting violent and attacking people after their marriage proposals have been turned down. A few cases have even resulted in murder.

A leading counselling firm that works with many BPO firms categorizes the problems, with which associates approach them, in the following buckets:

1. Work related: These account for 12 per cent of the problems. They have to do with career growth, performance issues, etc.
2. Self-related: These account for 25 per cent of the problems. They involve issues with self-confidence, shyness, loneliness, feeling left out in a crowd.
3. Relationship problems: These account for 50 per cent of the problems faced by BPO employees. Workplace romances, multiple partners, conflict with parents are the various relationship problems faced by them.
4. Others: These account for 13 per cent of the problems. They involve parenting, child care, finances, etc.

This ties in well with the behavioural pattern of the youth. They are action-oriented. They want to be visible and make an impact.

Myths and Realities of BPOs

A negative image of the BPO industry has been created by the press. When you have an industry or business where the average age of the employees is 21–22 years, there are bound to be behavioural problems. A night-shift job, freedom, and money at hand, compounds the problems. People in the industry are not promiscuous and live the life they like to lead. They are adults and can decide what they want to do.

We met and spoke with a large number of people working and wanting to work in the BPO industry. What was apparent was that for the majority it was a bridge job and not a career choice. People who have stayed on for more than two years and moved on to the role of TL tend to stay on and build a career in the BPO industry. Associates who keep job-hopping every six months burn out as they are never able to rise up the rungs and become managers.

We summarize here some of the interesting observations we made while talking with people working in BPO firms and those eager to join them.

Why do you want to join a BPO?

It is easy to get a job. Nobody is worried about a candidate's qualifications or marks. This is one of the few industries that hires freshers, whereas most other sectors want experienced candidates.

Do you plan to work long in a BPO?

The answer was a unanimous no. More than 80 per cent indicated that they saw a BPO job as a stepping-stone to other careers. Some girls wanted to become air-hostesses and felt that this was a good training ground. Others wanted to be independent and not ask parents for help. The BPO industry was a good place to earn some money. There were a few who wanted to save money for higher studies. Engineers joining the BPO industry felt that they would be able to get into a software job and these people wanted to join a large player doing both IT and BPO.

How do you spend your money?

Most people spend all that they earn in less than 15 days. Many seek salary advances. Credit card companies are challenged with large defaults from youngsters in the BPO industry who spend well beyond their capacity. Many of them are not aware that by paying the minimum due they are building up a huge interest penalty on the default, thereby pushing themselves into a debt trap. Dining out with friends, spending weekends out of town, frequent pubbing, and spending a lot of time in malls and plush stores buying branded clothes, shoes, perfumes, cosmetics, and other high-end accessories seems to be a common habit of the majority. Cell phone spends per month are more than Rs 500 and it is common for these youngsters to change their cell phones every year.

The common perception about BPO companies amongst industry outsiders is negative. Some of this may be true, but most of it can be attributed to the image created by the press. Some of these are:

1. It is very easy to get a job in a BPO company. You can walk in to any BPO firm and walk out with an offer letter.
2. The easy money that this industry provides and lack of tight controls spoils the lifestyle of the youth.
3. It is a night job and so is not safe for girls. Any girl working in a BPO company is of loose character.
4. There is too much of a party culture in the BPO industry. The people are not intellectually stimulated. Companies encourage a party culture.
5. Many companies do not deliver what they commit. The security lapses can be expensive.
6. Travel at night is not safe. Cars and vans working for BPO firms travel recklessly causing many accidents.
7. The typical image of a BPO employee that of a 21-year-old, with pierced ears, pony tail, faded jeans, a person who smokes and drinks, and has tasted drugs.

The reality is somewhere in between.

Getting a job in a good BPO company is not easy. Selection criteria are stringent and for every 100 people who apply, less than 10 are offered jobs. The interview and selection process involves multiple rounds and tests. But yes, it is true that most BPO companies are on a perpetual hiring spree and this is the only industry where you can walk in and out with a job offer the very same day.

The BPO industry is not the only one that has night jobs—the printing press, hotels, airlines, hospitals, and railways have people working in night shifts and this has been going on for decades.

The salary for any night-shift job is higher than that for an equivalent day-shift job and this may be attributed to the hardship involved. The 20 per cent higher salary needs to be looked upon as a hardship allowance.

Over 25,000 vehicles ply at night ferrying 600,000 people. Statistically, the number of accidents do not fall in any deviation bracket. There will be the odd accident at night as at night the roads are freer, there is no heavy traffic, and, as a result, there is a tendency to travel at higher speeds.

India has less than 1 per cent of the world's road vehicles and accounts for 6 per cent of road accidents. In India, one person dies every six minutes and 10 are injured in the same time due to road accidents. Yet, every accident involving the BPO industry makes headline news for the wrong reasons.

Notwithstanding this, there is a need for safety. As companies improve on their systems, individuals also need to be cautious. We would recommend the following steps for every individual, especially women travelling at night:

1. Women employees should ensure that they are not the first person in the car.
2. If there is a person before you, please ask him for his identity card/process and confirm that he is a company employee or an authorized security guard. Check the date of validity in the identity card.
3. In the car, avoid engaging in dialogue with the driver or the security guard.
4. Avoid talking on the phone while in the car. Be alert.
5. Keep your cell phone in your hand and configure a one-button dial to a friend just in case you need to make an emergency call.
6. Insist on not being the last person in the car while being dropped. Request a male colleague or guard to be with you.
7. If you need to walk to your house through a dark alley, ask the guard to accompany you.

8. If you are staying alone at home, ask the guard to wait till you enter the house and switch on the lights.
9. On reaching call your friends/relatives and inform them about your safe arrival.
10. It may help to keep a bottle of pepper spray with you.

While systems do exist they need to be adhered to even under normal conditions. Companies also need to improve on the following areas:

1. Work with transport and security agencies that have the capability to grow, have size and credibility. Do not pick the cheapest option.
2. Ensure that a background check is done for all employees sourced through a vendor/partner and provide them with an identity card. Since driver attrition is large, the identity card should be valid for only one month.
3. Have a 24x7 toll-free in-house call centre where people can call in for verification. The helpline should have sufficient lines and operators so that it is accessible immediately in an emergency.
4. All drivers working at night should be checked with breath analyser to ensure that they are not in an inebriated state.
5. All calls to employees should be made by the company's representatives. Employees' phone numbers should not be shared with drivers/transport vendors.
6. If employees do not reach work, the company's call centre must call them. (Most companies assume that the missing employees have taken the day off or have resigned.) Similarly, people, especially women, need to be called after it is confirmed that they have been dropped home.
7. Companies need to check and maintain valid telephone numbers of their employees and their guardians. This database needs to be refreshed frequently.
8. Companies that can afford should look at a GPRS solution with a panic alert system to track vehicles.

Most importantly, companies need to look at the process for safety and night travel as a Six Sigma project and identify areas that need to be measured, the service level agreements (SLAs), and the reporting mechanism. Many companies do not have a well-defined system that can be reviewed and measured on a daily basis for compliance.

Not enough has been highlighted about the perks and benefits that youngsters working in a BPO company enjoy. It has no parallel in any other industry. If you just list down all the benefits of working in the BPO industry, it does make it a compelling proposition:

1. BPO companies provide a good starting salary. Even an undergraduate can earn over Rs 100,000 (US$ 2,500) per year and if he is a capable and good performer, his salary curve can zoom 10 times in less than five years. That is a compounded growth of over 35 per cent every year.

2. They offer the convenience of home pick up and drop facilities. This is a service that is offered in very few industries. And it costs companies over Rs 4,000 per month per employee to arrange pick up and drop facilities. Many companies have even started offering air-conditioned cars. Most companies provide security to female employees.

3. BPO companies provide an excellent workplace. They provide fully air-conditioned, neat and clean cubicles and well-stocked cafeteria that works 24x7. Once you are inside a BPO you feel no difference between India, US, or Singapore. Most people take this for granted, but setting up and maintaining such world-class facilities costs money. Compare this work environment to that of a civil engineer, or an entry-level engineer working in the sweltering conditions of a steel plant.

4. Health and insurance cover and PF.

5. Reimbursement of higher education costs.

6. Soft loans and salary advances.

7. Discount deals on cell phones and credit cards are organized through the company.

8. Performance-linked bonus.
9. Retention bonus.
10. Getting an opportunity to hone your skills as a manager in two–three years.
11. A positive environment with lots of training, off-site meetings, and get-togethers are part of most good BPO firms.
12. Most importantly, any individual who has spent a few years in a BPO company comes out as a confident extrovert with excellent communication skills.

These are just some of the key benefits that BPO companies shower on their employees. Chances are that very few peer industries would be offering similar benefits.

Many of these benefits are used wrongly, which is what forces company management to tighten its strings. A BPO company in New Delhi observed that in July, August, and September, their ratio of women being hired went up steeply. Against an average 30–35 per cent ratio, it stood at 50 per cent. Through cafeteria talk and comments heard between friends in the training room, the company was able to figure out that many of the new hires were potential brides, about to get married in the peak wedding season of November and December. They were using the company as a paid training ground to brush up their English.

Confused Generation

A high disposable income with no responsibility can influence the spending pattern of any individual. And it is happening with the young workforce in the BPO industry.

In the BPO industry, the average age of employees is below 22 years and most of them are fresh out of college. They tend to spend money on lifestyle products and also spend a lot on social events. Many of them do not think of saving and try to imitate the lifestyle of the west. It is definitely affecting the BPO workforce.

We call the young BPO professionals confused, but their behaviour is in keeping with that of their peers in any other developed country. We are not familiar with this phenomenon in India and hence we label them a confused generation. But as they take up responsibility in life, their outlook to life changes with time. They gradually come to recognize the tricks and treats of earning money. Increasingly, we will see the younger generation moving out of their homes and start living on their own. This will definitely change the landscape of the social structure.

Many people joining the industry come from small towns. In trying to keep up with the peers, they end up getting addicted to a lifestyle of rampant clubbing and shopping. Very soon they realize that their expenses far exceed their income. This results not only in job-hopping, but also in credit card frauds.

These incidents are not myths, but realities across call centres. It affects not only freshers, but even married couples. The rate of divorce in call centres is increasing.

Such incidents have resulted in parents being concerned about their children working in the BPO industry. This is probably the reason why the Indian contact centre industry has less than 30 per cent women employees.

Too many options can actually confuse any individual. And this is exactly what is happening to the BPO workforce. Until recently, Indians were not comfortable with frequent job changes. The 'old generation' workforce believed in job security. In the 1960s, a government job was the best option. Today, anybody who wants to earn good money will want to take up a BPO job.

The environment is changing very fast. Very few people from the 'new generation' workforce think of retiring from the organization they are presently working in.

Our parents grew up in a system where they lived to take care of their parents and their children. Every penny was saved and the average middle-class family used to save up to 30 per cent of the monthly income. Loans were not available and buying a television set or a fridge was an aspiration for which you saved for months. This generation believed that when you are faced with challenges, you learn to overcome them better. They also believed that the taste of success is very sweet. They brought up their children with strong family and social values. Indians who struggled in the 1970s and 1980s have now established themselves.

When you know that you can get a job at 18, the motivation to study takes a backseat. Is the current generation having it too easy? Is this good for the future? Are we creating a generation of youngsters who think only of the present? Are they building skills and competencies that will steer them to a bright future? What will be their market potential 20 years from now?

Indeed, the BPO industry has helped grow several ancillary activities. Nearly 70 per cent of the people joining a BPO firm leave the industry within two years. Many have moved to the airlines industry, to the hospitality industry, to retail, and to other service industries. Jobs are being offered on a platter these days.

The rigour of metrics and measurement has made the BPO job a transaction job bereft of emotions. You service a customer who you do not see and in most cases you do not understand their culture. How do you correlate with such a customer? This is a paradox since the cornerstones of the BPO industry are service and empathy.

Will these youngsters be able to survive if the bubble bursts? And it does not take too long for a slowdown to happen. In today's global economy, if the US sneezes, India catches a cold. The rush for profit has made us a country of traders. The BPO business in its current state is based on a pure labour arbitrage model. What happens to the hundreds of thousands if the industry slows down?

We have in earlier sections indicated the meteoric rise and career growth of many people in the industry. If a slowdown hits the industry what will be the impact on the entry-level staff? With the playing field shrinking, jobs will reduce and so will attrition. Growth opportunities will minimize. How long can an agent keep taking calls? Currently, people max out after attending to calls for two–three years. In the event of a recession, there is the danger of people being stuck on the floor taking calls for much longer periods.

This is not a pessimistic prediction, but a reality, which may hit the industry anytime soon. The great recession in the US and the revolution in France have had long-lasting social and political impacts.

Indians by nature are not the most creative entrepreneurs. They are good at replication. The first mall in India came up in Gurgaon, a suburb of New Delhi in 2002. Since then hundreds have sprouted all over the country. National Highway 8 and the Mumbai–Pune Highway were the first international class roads that came up in India in the early 2000s. Since then thousands of miles of roads have been added. There were only a handful of BPO companies in the early 2000s; today we have in excess of 5,000 BPO companies with no major differences in parameters that distinguish one from the other.

A quick comparison with the US, Japan, and Israel indicates that an economy built on the foundation of individual creativity grows faster and in a healthier manner.

The BPO environment is transaction based. You are required to follow processes and rules, again and again. Execution has to be done without questioning.

By doing this is the BPO industry churning out a generation of youth who have stopped thinking and rationalizing? Will this

Figure 4.3: Fifty Career Growth Options in a BPO

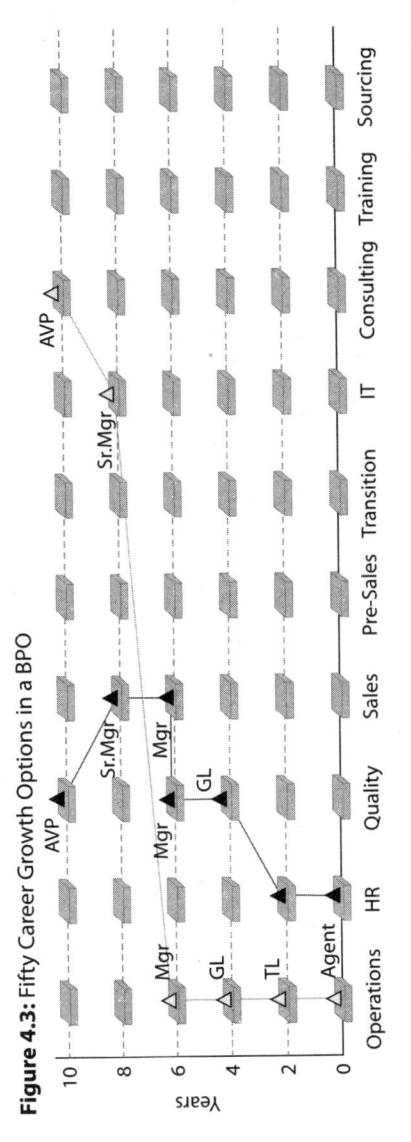

impact the country in the future? This is a scary thought, which most people seem to forget in the midst of frenetic growth.

However, with all these challenges what makes a job in the BPO industry compelling is the choice of over 50 different career options during a 10-year duration (see Figure 4.3). There are many examples of successful people who have gone on to become general managers (GMs) in 10–12 years. Compare this with the fact that it take more than 25 years to become a GM in the government sector. And a GM in the BPO industry earns more than twice what a GM in the government sector does.

No other industry can offer such a wide variety of roles. This is a compelling reason for people to look at this as a career and not a stop-gap job. Fast-paced growth and steep remuneration jumps make it one of the most exciting and promising places to be in. The industry looks at rotating people and giving them career growth. Figure 4.3 shows the 10 tracks for growth over the years, assuming a promotion every 18–24 months. It is easy to understand how a stint in the BPO industry can open up 50 different career paths over a 10-year period. *And most importantly, this is one industry that can stake a claim of people being able to reach the Rs 1 million salary mark within 1,500 days of starting a job. And there are thousands who have achieved this dream.*

There are many examples of how people who have joined the BPO industry have moved faster. If after graduation, a student joined the BPO industry and his batch-mate from the class of 2000 joined a manufacturing firm or a bank and stayed put in the same job for seven years, chances are that the person who joined the BPO industry would be far ahead both in terms of remuneration and responsibility.

CHAPTER 5

The Future of BPOs

It has been a glorious run till now, but what does the future look like for the Indian BPO industry? Will the bull run continue? Are there risks looming around the horizon? We share here a quick summary of what is in store for the future.

There is unanimous consensus that in the next five years, the BPO market in India will continue to grow at a compound annual growth rate (CAGR) of 30–40 per cent. This will result in a market that could exceed revenues of US$ 20 billion by 2012. A large share of that, in excess of US$ 10 billion will come from the knowledge process outsourcing (KPO) or high-end business. With revenues of US$ 20 billion, the industry would employ in excess of 1.5 million people.

Take a deep breath. The numbers we are talking here mean that in the next five years, the industry will achieve three times what it has in the last seven years. That is a colossal achievement, which probably has no parallel in the global industry.

For pessimists who think this is too far-fetched a dream, the reality is that with revenues of US$ 20 billion in 2012, we would have just 10 per cent of the global BPO market share. That is surely achievable.

This is the dream that is fuelling the growth strategy of every company. The strategy of most companies will be to focus on the vast non-voice business. Companies that started out as pure voice players, struggling with low profits and high attrition, see the transaction processing industry as a more profitable and scaleable model.

The Indian market is predominantly dependent on the United States (US). Corporations in the US love India for the cost benefit it provides, but their comfort level with Canada, Mexico, and even South America is higher.

Our predictions are based on what we have heard from industry leaders and the trends we have seen across the globe. We have spoken to industry leaders, customers, analysts, and consultants, and then arrived at what we feel are 15 clear directions for the business. All our predictions come with a five-year window.

70–30 Rule

Large successful companies will have 70 per cent of their business from non-voice operations and 30 per cent from voice operations. This mirrors the global trend and the size of the business to be outsourced. A large BPO company five years from today would be earning revenues to the tune of more than US$ 1 billion. We anticipate that at least five Indian players will reach that scale of operations in the next five years. This growth will happen with 30–40 per cent organic growth, while the rest will happen through inorganic growth.

With a total revenue of US$ 1 billion, a 30 per cent voice component would measure up to revenues of US$ 300 million. That is massive. The voice business will not necessarily be low cost. High-end technical support and the diagnostics call centre business will command a premium rate and the rate will be higher than many transaction processing activities.

80–20 Rule: The Big Will Get Bigger

It is inevitable that the big will get bigger. If we look at the information technology (IT) market, the top six, namely, Tata Consultancy Service (TCS), Wipro, Infosys, Satyam, Cognizant, and Hindustan Computers Limited (HCL) contribute to more than 80 per cent of the total revenue earned by the Indian IT companies. Today, the top six in BPO contribute less than 25 per cent of the revenues. The BPO trend will mirror the IT trend. Customer deals are getting larger and they see comfort and security in partnering with the big players. The strengthening of the rupee will also put pressure on the smaller players.

It is easier for the big to get bigger. The strong growth of the BPO industry made some entrepreneurs quite wealthy in the initial days, but the market today is slowly getting controlled by the big daddies. Barring Genpact and WNS, all the other large Indian players are IT-BPO companies.

Integrated IT-BPO business seems to be the trend. Although the customer interface for IT (chief information officer [CIO]) is different from that of BPO (customer service, chief finance officer [CFO] or operations team), large Fortune 500 companies are coming out with integrated request for proposals (RFPs) for total outsourcing projects. This gives an undue advantage to integrated IT-BPO companies.

As labour arbitrage ceases to be a differentiator and companies focus on benefits from optimization, large companies with consulting divisions will stand to gain. Companies will want to improve the process before outsourcing. Consulting arms with in-depth domain knowledge will help customers achieve this.

Captives have a cost structure that is 40 per cent higher than third-party players. The size of third-party players and their share will be larger than those of captives. The current 50–50 mix will change to a 70–30 mix in favour of third-party vendors.

Shared Services Centres

Shared services centres are not dedicated to one client. They utilize the bandwidth of their trained manpower to offer services to a range of customers from the same industry. This is a true example of a back office factory. Shared services centres have seen a lot of success in Europe.

Shared services centres for transaction processing will grow by leaps and bounds. This will be a business-driven growth to maintain productivity and profitability. If you have one customer for whom you do accounts payable work, the agent may at best process five or six bills a day. That would take two or three hours of his time. Other examples of shared services work could be managing the payroll or income tax returns for a corporation, or doing back-end paralegal work, equity and company research.

The basis for this is multiplexing of your team to ensure better dynamic load balancing. Normally for dedicated customers, you plan your staff for peak loads. In the lull period, there is a lot of productivity loss. A shared services centre will manage multiple customers and work on a transaction-based pricing.

A shared services centre will not have leading edge work, but will process rule-based operations that are similar across corporations. This will help in setting up the first tier of the back office. Most shared services centres are set up by multinational corporations since it avoids the hassles of confidentiality.

However, there are large third-party players in this space as well.

It is a win–win situation for both the customer and the service provider since the customer will see a 15–20 per cent lower price.

Global Centres

A successful BPO firm would need to cover the globe. Large deals are not just integrated IT-BPO deals, but are also transnational. An RFP from Microsoft or General Motors would need the partner to offer services in over 25 languages in more than 50 countries. Presence in each continent will become a mandatory requirement. As a starting point, companies must have a centre in China, east Europe, South America, and Mexico in addition to India and maybe the Philippines. Along with this, we will also see the globalization of BPO companies. More than 25 per cent of employees will be non-Indians. The human resources (HR) head of the company will in all probability be a person who has been in a multinational corporation managing operations in multiple countries.

Spanish is the most commonly spoken language after English. It is spoken in over 24 countries. This provides an opportunity for countries like Mexico and Argentina, which are low-cost hubs, to run operations for Spanish-speaking customers.

Integration will happen and we will see more foreigners operating from Indian shores. A study by Evalueserve indicated that by 2010, over 160,000 foreign language professionals would be needed in the Indian IT/BPO industry. Of these 40,000 would be Indians who have trained themselves, the remaining would be foreigners.

TeamLease, India's largest temporary staffing company, has been witnessing an increase in interest from foreign students who come down to India to study in universities such as New Delhi's Jawaharlal Nehru University, Bangalore University, and the Chennai-based Anna University.

Many foreigners are lured by the attraction of living in a country that is increasingly viewed by the overseas media as a dynamic nation. What better way of living in and experiencing a nation than to work in the BPO industry? The experience also looks good on a curriculum vitae (CV).

How are foreigners allowed to work in India? Obtaining a visa is not difficult because Indian rules and regulations are far more relaxed than, say, those of the US.

BPO companies have been hiring foreigners mainly in three specific areas—training, transaction and migration processes, and in quality management.

In order for a process to get transitioned, training is required. Instead of sending 150 Indians overseas, the parent company or the client sends someone for a period of six months to a year.

There is little doubt too that Indian BPO companies have steadily been winning more and more business from European companies. This has led to the growing importance of multilingual capabilities, both in voice and data operations.

Today, the Indian BPO industry offers services in multilingual capability—French, Spanish, German, Japanese, and Italian. Industry observers claim that BPO companies in some cities seem to be zeroing in on specific language—German dominates Mumbai, Italian and Russian dominate New Delhi, Japanese is dominant in Chennai, and French in Bangalore and Pondicherry.

Companies save on training costs as these employees can start functioning from the first day. These employees get a chance to work and get an opportunity to see the country. There are many youngsters abroad who see this as a paid holiday in a fast-growing foreign country.

Though the cost of hiring foreigners is perhaps not low, BPO companies would have had to fork out more on training a huge number of Indians in foreign languages.

This is truly the beginning of global integration of the workforce and BPO companies can take full credit for getting this phase started.

Onsite Placements

At least 30–40 per cent of revenues of IT companies come from onsite billing. For most BPO companies, 100 per cent of the revenue is from offshore billing. This is set to change; the staff augmentation market is big. The salary for a call centre agent in India is US$ 3000 per annum while in Denmark it is over US$ 40,000. The same is the case for an entry-level accountant. A difference in salary structure that is 10 times cheaper is an opportunity to build a profitable business in onsite staffing.

The brain drain of the 1960s and the 1970s formed the basis for work getting outsourced to India in the 1980s and 1990s. The credibility and trust of Indian managers who had excelled in US corporations was the basis on which the initial outsourcing contracts were signed.

The workforce in global BPO companies is large—not only can these companies engage in large-scale staff augmentation programmes, many consultants can look at this as a business model to place Indian BPO staff abroad.

There is also an opportunity for companies to set up shop in small towns in the US. The cost structure in Dakota, Nebraska, or Albuquerque is not very different from that in Mumbai or New Delhi. Employing locals and running a near shore centre will mean a full 360 degree turn in the history of outsourcing.

Issues regarding visa availability, acceptability of Indian workforce in large numbers, minimum salary levels, are things that need to be sorted out. Given the dearth of talent in many countries, especially in west Europe, there is a distinct possibility of this trend becoming a reality.

Platform

Most of the work in the transaction processing space is rule based and repeatable. This can get automated through a platform. A future Bill Gates could come up with an innovative solution to eliminate manpower and get the rule-based work done through a platform.

In HR, BPO companies have already started seeing this trend where payroll, 401 K, and other benefits are being driven through a platform strategy. Companies like Fidelity have invested millions in setting up platforms. Investment in platforms is large and this is where the integrated IT-BPO story can make a strong value proposition.

Support.com, a company that has been developing automation tools had evolved a model by which the technical helpdesk business could reduce the cost of resolution from a high of US$ 257 per resolution (for a site visit by an engineer) to a low of less than US$ 1 (through predictive diagnostics and sniffer tools). Many of the remote diagnostic solutions used in high-end mainframes and UNIX servers can be brought down to personal computers (PCs) and handheld devices. Self-service is clearly the direction for the future (see Figure 5.1).

Salary Bubble May Erupt

The salary bubble may erupt. With consolidation of the industry and entry barriers for newcomers being high, there will be a

Figure 5.1: Effect of Platform on BPO

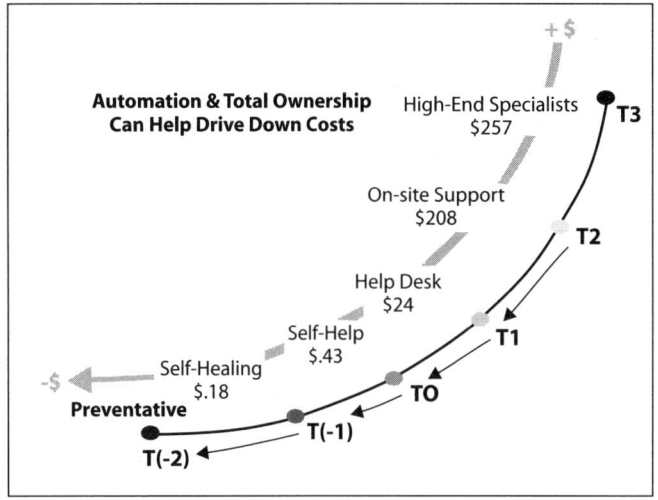

Source: Support Soft product presentation.

rationalization in salaries paid in the BPO industry. Annual pay packet increases of 30–40 per cent will be history. Very soon the industry will realize that they are pricing themselves out of the market. The China threat will force Indian companies to look at the galloping salary costs.

Attrition Will Come Down

As the industry matures and leading players/brands establish themselves, the attrition rate in the industry will come down. It will not reach the attrition rates of IT companies that stand at 12–20 per cent, but will still be in a manageable 30–40 per cent level. Lower attrition will pay for more competitive rates.

The attrition in the non-voice business is today less than 30 per cent. With non-voice operations contributing to over 75 per cent of the BPO market, it will help get overall attrition down.

Concepts like temping, part-time employment, and work from home will catch up. Attrition in this segment is very low.

As the large companies grow rapidly, tenured employees will see speedy career growth. BPO jobs will start becoming career options—especially with the expansion of BPO companies to smaller cities to feed the voracious appetite for talent.

The industry will mature and work towards solving grass-root problems. It will work towards achieving realistic performance targets, which will reduce stress. The left and unions will provide constructive guidelines to streamline the working conditions of this large workforce. All this will reduce stress and hence attrition.

The initial work being done by a few companies towards achieving higher conversion ratios in up-market locations will fructify. Finishing schools, reformed college curriculum, and BPO-focused training institutes and courses will help add thousands to the list of employable workforce. All this will result in lowering the attrition rates.

BPO Cities Will Emerge

Integrated townships/special economic zones (SEZs), which have offices, houses, dormitory accommodation, shopping centres, and medical facilities will emerge. This will minimize travel and commute time. This will emerge in second and third tier towns. Some may even come up in campus cities like Anand in Gujarat and Manipal in Karnataka. The BPO companies will allow students to work part-time and pay for their education.

The cities will operate on a 24x7 time clock that will match with the industry.

When integrated steel plants were set up in the 1960s in Rourkela, Bhilai, Durgapur, and Bokaro, a similar concept was used and integrated townships were developed. This helped fuel the local economy. There are already numerous developers in Metro Manila who have already planned to set up integrated townships.

The cost of infrastructure in metro cities like Mumbai and New Delhi will make it difficult to afford setting up BPO centres there. Do not be surprised if by 2012 all BPO companies have moved from Mumbai to Lonawala. We predict that banking majors will set up their back office centres with large capacities in smaller cities like Jamnagar. It will not take too long for these predictions to become a reality.

Temping Will Catch Up

Globally, 40 per cent of the employees in the BPO industry are temporary, staffed through temping agencies. The agency hires, trains, and deploys people. In case of attrition, it is their responsibility to provide a replacement. In the recent past, we have seen some captives trying this model. A leading multinational corporation (MNC) bank recently floated an RFP. One clause in this RFP was that it was the responsibility of the service provider to provide a replacement in case of attrition. This was contested by leading Indian BPO players. This clause was a smart move and we can expect this trend to be replicated more frequently.

Not just temping, but recruitment process outsourcing (RPO) will soon catch up as a cost-effective solution, which brings in predictability on hiring numbers to companies. The basis of outsourcing has been to focus on core competencies, and companies today spend an enormous amount of time trying to meet their staffing requirements. RPO is globally a Rs 27 billion market and is yet to make an impact in the Indian industry.

Along with temping, one can also see the growth of people working from home. Good telecom infrastructure will facilitate this. We have seen this trend getting started in the US where a few airline companies have tried this successfully. If this takes off in India it can be a boom.

Investment in IT Tools and Technology

Companies will need to invest significantly in IT systems. Enterprise resource planning (ERP), workforce management (WFM), and data warehousing tools will be essential for companies to manage a global workforce and eliminate subjectivity. These tools will pay for themselves with reduced manpower.

Self-service, predictability tools, and remote diagnostics will help companies resolve customer problems faster.

With the spread of 3G wideband CDMA, today's telephonic calls may soon become video calls. This will radically change the approach of customer service as communication with video would be a lot easier.

Do Not Ignore the Domestic Market

Do not ignore the domestic market. Every large MNC is looking at India for the long haul, be it Wal-Mart or General Motors. Bill Gates and Sam Palisamo are not making multiple trips to India for sight-seeing. Wipro and HCL, the domestic

IT giants of the 1980s and the 1990s ignored the local market and tried to make their fortune in the US. Some of the largest system integration deals in the recent past have happened in India. The Bharti–IBM or the Bank of India–Hewlett-Packard (HP) deal run into hundreds of millions of dollars. It is a contradiction that Indian giants like Wipro, Infosys, and TCS are not winning large deals in their own backyard.

Large BPO companies are clearly ignoring the Indian market since the deals today are not profitable. With a strengthening rupee this stand will change.

Managing large Indian operations gives you better seat utilization and helps you amortize the cost of infrastructure and support. The logic cannot be questioned, but why it is not happening is a mystery.

Washington Mutual is a large bank that works with some Indian partners. They outsource both IT and BPO operations. Both operations are run from the same facility in the same city, but from different buildings. It is baffling why they cannot use the same facility since the IT workforce could work during the day and the BPO workforce at night.

As companies struggle to improve their bottom line, innovative plans like these are more apt than trying to make people work on Saturdays and work for 10 hours a day.

The Indian telecom players and banks are reaching the scale and size of global players. Customers will demand services and outsourcing them is the best way. Since cost is a consideration, work will move to smaller towns and third-tier cities. A few large Indian corporate like HDFC have even started considering rural BPOs.

At Home Agents

At home agents are individuals who work from home in their free time and get paid on a transaction they complete. They are not full-time employees or temporary agents. There is a large, fast growing market for this. At last count, the US alone had over 100,000 at home agents working for different corporations. Jet Blue, a new airline which launched its service a few years back, adopted this model for its ticketing agents. Even Pizza Hut is said to have a large number of home agents.

The model is simple—individuals register as home agents and provide their phone numbers. Based on the area/zip code where they stay, the calls are routed to them. If they do not pick up the phone in two rings, it gets routed to the next agent. Once the agent takes a call, they complete a simple job like taking an order or booking a seat.

The domestic BPO industry has a huge potential for the home agent market not just for the call centre business, but for the transaction processing business as well.

176 Employee Database and Certification

The National Association of Software and Services Companies (NASSCOM) is working on creating a central database of BPO employees and a common test that can be used as a selection criteria for all BPO companies. This will simplify the selection procedure both in terms of time and cost of selection. Companies like MeritTrac are also following a similar approach through their TracSkill programme. A centralized database with employment records will become a reality very soon.

Chain Reactions

The eco-system to serve this industry will transform completely. Given the size and scale, many mom and pop shop operations will consolidate. Let us not be surprised if Hertz or Avis open a dedicated car service to cater to the BPO market. An integrated transport system of cars, vans, or even buses would operate for all BPO companies for a particular city. This would result in excellent capacity utilization. This service could run 24x7 across all the routes where BPO companies have offices.

Recruitment and training, which is highly fragmented with thousands of players, will consolidate with clear industry leaders offering RPO and turnkey solutions. The recruitment market for IT/BPO in 2007 was in excess of Rs 10 billion (US$ 250 million) and this would expand to an industry in excess of Rs 30 billion (US$ 750 million) by 2012. Associated services like assessment and background check would be industries supporting the recruitment industry.

Risks and Areas to Look Out For

Strong Rupee Will Impact Margins

A strengthening rupee can play havoc with profit margins. Between January and July 2007, the rupee gained by 9 per cent moving from Rs 46 to nearly Rs 40 against the US dollar. Industry experts say that this trend is unstoppable. Years of intervention by the Reserve Bank of India (RBI) has held up the rupee artificially. Given the growth of the economy and investments needed in infrastructure, foreign direct investment (FDI) is needed in billions. What flows into India is a fraction of what reaches China. Free market reforms and easing entry of FDI into diverse sectors will help the Indian market to grow at a 9–10 per cent rate for the next 5–10 years. This will result in further strengthening of the rupee. Estimates on the exchange rate between the US dollar and the Indian rupee range from 35–38.

Most BPO companies operate at a 9–15 per cent margin. This will get diluted with the rupee appreciating. Customers are not too keen to increase rates to help overcome the deficit. While the larger BPO companies will manage, the smaller BPO firms with 100 per cent dependency on the US market will find it difficult to survive. There are more than 400 BPO companies that operate in India; more than 300 of them have revenues less than US$ 50 million. It is these sub-US$ 100 million operations that face the highest risk of being wiped out. Seeing this trend, many smaller companies have already started selling and this trend will accelerate.

The government is in no mood to listen to the industry and provide sops and support. They have other Herculean challenges in the agricultural sector which have higher priority.

Unionization

The left is a strong force in the Indian government. The central government stands to lose majority without the support of the left parties. There have been strong murmurs in many cities, especially Kolkata, on the need to unionize the BPO employees and get them their rightful share. Lack of standard practices and strong government framework is resulting in a few companies running their operations like a sweat shop. Extending hours of work, not paying relevant dues in a timely manner, not providing basic facilities listed at the time of employment like leave, etc., are some of the complaints against the industry.

All this is true in part and the industry is to blame for this. These factors contribute to attrition.

The Philippines has a strong framework that ensures that employees get a fair deal. This has helped the industry. Industry leaders, however, feel that unionization will ring the death knell for the industry. Many companies have been hesitant to expand their operations in Kolkata and start new ones in Kerala—both places being under the direct governance of the left.

Backlash in the US

For every five jobs that are generated in Indian BPO companies, three people lose jobs in the US. While this is helping corporations save money and invest in new technology and products, there is no denying the fact that entry-level jobs are where 80 per cent of the employment happens in every country. The engineers and lawyers will find themselves jobs; it is the undergraduates and high school dropouts who are threatened by this surge of outsourcing.

The US companies have had a global hegemony for over 40 years. Trillion dollar debts, a weakening dollar, and a war that is dragging on are signs of recession around the corner.

Emerging Countries

If China gets its act in place, it can grow very rapidly in the BPO space. A disciplined workforce and excellent government support packaged with great infrastructure makes it a very attractive proposition. The cost structure in China will be at par or lower than India. Lack of English skills will limit the growth of English contact centres; the transaction processing industry is the one where China will make a big impact. Proximity to

Korea and Japan will also help them garner large business from these developed economies.

Platform

Anything which is manual and rule based can be executed through a platform. A set of sharp brains focusing on this will emerge as the next Microsoft or Google. The size of the market is large enough for someone to focus and emerge with the right solution. Automation is the biggest threat to the BPO industry. Intelligent self-help and predictive healing can wipe out the entire technical helpdesk business. Automatic voice response systems are already being used by many airline companies in the US.

Fraud and Security Glitches

It is fortunate that there have been no major instances in the recent past of fraud and security glitches. With the scale and size of the business increasing, companies have to invest in the latest technology to proactively ensure that there is no threat to data security. A few bad incidents can have a serious impact on the future of the business.

CHAPTER 6

Points to Ponder

In the previous chapters we have looked at the BPO industry from all angles. In this section we look at a different set of parameters that define the brand and value system of the BPO industry. We look at the framework and try to determine some of the key ingredients that are missing in the BPO industry, which today is in between a fast growing hot industry and a social drama. We compare the BPO industry with other industries to seek the commonalities and differences and to seek knowledge that will help us overcome the challenges faced by the BPO industry. We look at the fundamentals that need to be in place for any industry to grow.

Fathers of the Industry and Their Role

When you think of the information technology (IT) industry, you think of Narayana Murthy, Ramadorai, and Azim Premji—stalwarts who defined the industry and set the foundation for three of India's largest IT companies. All three have been closely associated with the industry right from day one and have been instrumental in shaping the industry and making it a force to be reckoned with at the global level.

When you think of BPO who do you think of? Who are the people who not just started and pioneered the industry, but are also actively involved in steering the industry and establishing a brand called Indian BPO. It is indeed difficult to find the parallels of Azim Premji and Narayana Murthy for the BPO industry.

An interesting observation is that as of January 2007, a majority of chief executive officers (CEOs) of BPO companies are either chartered accountants or bankers by profession. An immediate question that comes to mind is—are these analytical and number-oriented professionals limiting the visionary growth of the industry?

Unfortunately, the BPO industry lacks the fatherly touch of towering industry stalwarts. Given the status of the industry and challenges that it is facing, it desperately needs guidance and direction not just for meeting its growth numbers, but to define its character and personality and to define and establish its brand with a set of core values.

Corporate Values

Values, vision, promise, beliefs, mission—these statements adorn the walls of most corporate houses. Whenever there is a new CEO, his first job is to summon a leadership meet and have a workshop to decide on the road ahead and to create the guiding and operating principles for the organization. You need to make an impact in 90 days!

What is the impact of this exercise—is it skin deep or is it genuine? Does it stem from a short-term need or is it the central point around which the company can manoeuvre its growth? Is it a communication, or a public relations exercise, or does it go beyond that? How effective is it in today's corporations where we live quarter to quarter? Is there a difference in impact between a large corporation and a small one? Do companies practice what they pin up on their walls? Do CEOs really mean what they say in the public forums? Have the ideologies and best practices percolated down to the grass-root worker in a BPO? Is it touching their daily lives and making an impact? These are some questions that BPO companies need to ask themselves.

CEOs today have almost dictatorial powers. General Electric (GE) is one of the most successful companies in the world. Under Jack Welsh the company developed an aggressive culture and gave a long leash of independence to managers who delivered on their numbers. This did help the company to grow rapidly, but it also created a group of managers who were ruthless, arrogant, and successful. Is this the right approach? Does it pay in the long term to create managers who are measured only on performance? This trend is indeed debatable.

Creating a dream and communicating it to thousands of employees is a powerful way of uniting any group as a team. But most organizations struggle to create a dream and end up defining a revenue target as their goal. While this is easy to measure, it really does not charge up people in a company and ends up becoming the driver for the top 100 people in the corporation.

Start-ups have a dream. They attract people not with salaries and perks, but with the dream of creating something new and innovative. Money and success is an outcome of this dream. This dream motivates them to achieve often impossible goals. The journey is as exciting as the final result. Motivated employees stretch and deliver quality output. They look forward to come to work. They are passionate. They exude positive energy and this halo effect touches all the employees around them. They do not work with a gun to their head—they work because they love what they are doing.

The biggest disappointment for junior employees is when they see leaders not practicing what they preach. This is especially true in BPO companies. During open house and meet the CEO events, the speeches and audio-visual talk of an ideal organization where you have transparency and a solution to every problem. Junior employees often hear things about their organization like 'We are a listening organization', 'We work as a team and share the spoils', 'We don't compromise on integrity'. However, reality turns out to be very different. The people making these statements do not live up to what they say; rule makers have a different set of rules for themselves. When this happens employees very soon lose trust and faith in the leadership and in the organization.

Every quarter there is a reason for cost cutting—profits are low, the rupee is gaining strength, the competition is hotting up, deals in the pipeline do not look good. Sit through any meeting and you will find it hilarious to see the ideas tossed around about how to cut costs.

With the rupee gaining over 10 per cent in 2007, BPO board rooms would have witnessed cost-cutting ideas like 'Let us make the agents work on Saturdays', 'Let us increase the work time to 10 hours' , 'All transport vehicles must have five people, even if it means that people will need to spend longer time travelling', 'Remove the cafeteria subsidy'—this could go on and on. About 90 per cent of the suggestions talk about cutting cost at the entry level. Why are there no suggestions like 'No business class travel for senior management', 'Let us cut our hotel costs from Rs 10,000 a day to Rs 8,000 for the management', 'Let the top 100 employees take a 10 per cent pay cut'?

Cost cutting is good, but many managers have become obsessed about demonstrating their value and commitment to the company by being obedient and disciplined in the art of cost cutting. The result is that the management becomes penny wise, but pound foolish. Employees often joke that the chief financial officer (CFO) should be re-designated as the CCO or the chief cost-cutting officer.

If the average salary hike in the company is 15 per cent, what should be the hike of the CEO and the top management? Common sense says 15 per cent. Check out India's leading IT/BPO companies and you will find that the top 100 employees in the hierarchy enjoy hikes that are higher than the company average. It is also a time to reflect on the gap between the entry-level salaries and those paid at the highest level. The entry-level salary is Rs 120,000 (US$ 3,000) per annum and the top management's salary ranges between Rs 7.5 and Rs 10 million (US$ 187,500–250,000) per annum. That is, the top management draws a salary 60 times that of the entry-level worker. Internationally, salaries would range from US$ 30,000 for the entry level to US$ 300,000 for the top management—a 10-fold gap.

The questions that come to mind on seeing such variations are: Are decision-makers and top managers doling out fancy perks for themselves while making the lower level struggle? Is it a case of the rich becoming richer? Does this trend augur well for the companies in the long run?

The churn in BPO firms adds to the complexity of building values. How do you build values when the attrition is close to 100 per cent? It is not only at the entry level, but even at the middle and senior management levels that the attrition rates are horrendously high.

Most corporations groom people for marathon stints; in the BPO industry it is different. If a person is retained for two years, then there is no regret about losing him.

The challenge of value system again seems to be a self-imposed problem and needs proactive steps from market leaders to fix it.

Most great organizations have grown on a foundation of values. They have hired people with similar values, trained them and ensured that this core aspect of the company is not lost out amidst the pandemonium of growth. This is crucial and many Indian companies, especially the BPO companies seem to be missing out on this.

People in any organization can be categorized into four buckets (see Figure 6.1):

1. Brilliant–simple.
2. Brilliant–arrogant.
3. Mediocre–simple.
4. Mediocre–arrogant.

Figure 6.1: People Profile in an Organization

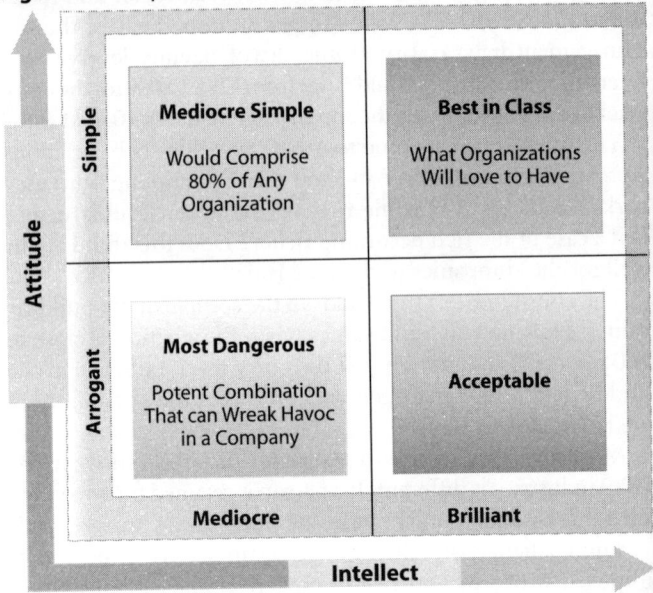

Great organizations are built with brilliant–simple people. Narayana Murthy and Azim Premji are the perfect examples of brilliant–simple people who set the foundation for the Indian IT industry and transformed the lives of millions.

Our generation would have seen a very different India if not for these two gentlemen who along with Tata Consultancy

Service (TCS) slowly and silently created a juggernaut which stands tall globally on all parameters.

The challenge is with arrogant–mediocrity. It is easy to identify this crowd. They typically stay in the same role for a long time, do not develop a second in line, and have high levels of insecurity. Their strategy in every meeting is to confuse and spread the deliverables over multiple groups. They shudder from accountability.

Arrogant–mediocrity hurts an organization. Companies with arrogant and mediocre leaders will not sustain themselves in the long term. A company which has a majority of senior people in this category is in serious trouble. Arrogant mediocre leaders make the organization weak and hollow.

Cheap versus Value for Money

Every large corporation needs to choose a core strategy from amongst the following three pivots:

1. Innovation.
2. Customer service.
3. Operational efficiency.

Product companies like 3M, Intel, Cisco, and Apple have innovation as their core value. They constantly need to launch new products with new features at attractive prices.

Singapore Airlines and Shangri La Hotels, and even Oberoi, Taj, and Jet Airways in India are examples of companies in the travel and hospitality industry that have customer service as their core competence. Dell and Federal Express have built their engines on a platform of operational efficiency.

While a company may take one of the pivots as the basis and score a 10 out of 10 on it, it has to do equally well on the other two parameters and score at least a 7 on them to maintain competitiveness.

What is the core competency of the Indian IT/BPO companies? It is clearly not innovation—with Accenture and IBM setting up a large base in India, the labour arbitrage advantage that Indian companies enjoyed for the last 15 years is fast disappearing.

Innovation although talked about has not been the core focus of Indian companies. And they have limited success stories to write home about.

The platforms of Six Sigma and SEI CMM did create the foundation for operational efficiency, but very soon it transformed to ruthless cost cutting.

Can operational efficiency and cost cutting be the core strategy? Can this be the engine which drives you to growth from US$ 7 billion to US$ 30 billion? This is a debatable point. Shombit Sengupta in his book, *Jalebi Management* says that 'Operational efficiency is like a spring—if you stretch, it very soon becomes a wire.'

An Olympus camera purchased in Singapore would ordinarily cost US$ 400. However, the same item is sold at US$ 250 at Best Buy during its Christmas sale. That is a deal, that is value for money. Wal-Mart delivers value for money on every item it sells. That is a promise the company makes—'More for less' and it ensures that this promise is delivered in all its transactions.

Deccan Airlines started as a low-cost airlines in India. Its brand proposition was low cost, no frills airlines. Yes, it is the lowest on fares, but there is no predictability with the airlines. It is routine to see its flights delayed by four to five hours, customer service agents have no answers for customers, flights get cancelled in the blink of an eye as customers are aggregated in common flights, and refunds are not available at airport counters. Fares are announced at Re 1 and you later come to know that the tax component is more than Rs 1,000. Overall it is an experience that most passengers would not want to put themselves through. People who travel by air do so because it gets them to a destination faster than a train.

Southwest Airlines runs a no frill, low-cost airlines in the US. They have the best website, the most responsive call centre, and the best records for flights being on time. The crew is professional and witty. They have the best schemes to attract frequent business travellers. They are the cheapest airlines, but people who have travelled with them once keep coming back again and again. Southwest Airlines makes more profit than the full service United or American airlines.

The difference is simple, Southwest Airline provides value for money while Deccan is cheap. Southwest Airlines has survived and grown over the years. It has repeat customers who love the airlines. Air Deccan is already going bust, and if Kingfisher had not bailed it out it would have been in serious trouble.

Indian BPO companies need to decide if they want to emulate Deccan Airlines or Southwest Airlines.

Love Affair with the Stock Markets

India's frenzy with the stock market is a decade-old phenomena. Every quarter during earning season, the corporate office literally comes to a standstill for a full week as preparations are in full swing to demonstrate how you have done better than the previous quarter. Frequently asked questions (FAQs) are prepared, the press is wooed, and the best people are put forward to make the right statements to ensure that the company's stock moves in the right direction.

Is the success of a company measured purely by the price to earnings ratio and the stock price? Normal thinking says that if you are in the right business, are innovative, run an efficient shop, take good care of your employees, and invest for the future, then the company will do well. And this reflects in your stock price.

Most companies—and many BPO companies—define success by the profits made at the end of the quarter. Call centres worldwide make 12–13 per cent earnings before interest, depreciation, taxes, and amortization (EBIDTA). If you have a good mix of transaction processing work, you can stretch that to 15–18 per cent.

Given this scenario, if you see that a company has a profit margin of 25 per cent, and you also observe that it has a large call centre concentration, one of the highest attrition rates, and its employees are amongst the lowest paid, then what do you infer? Is the company doing a miraculous job or is it squeezing its resources, which cannot be sustained in the long run?

It is easy to spot the reason behind this. Most CEOs have salary packets that are linked to their performance. Many CEOs also keep changing their roles every two or three years. Their modus operandi is to join the company, create high visibility, show some short-term changes, and to get out of the organization before the down side of these short-term changes starts emerging.

Customers clearly see a difference in behaviour with regard to companies that get listed. Sobha Builders is a name to reckon with in Bangalore. Over the years, the company has built a solid reputation of delivering quality homes in a timely manner. People who have purchased multiple units from Sobha over the years have indicated a significant difference in the behaviour of the company post its initial public offer (IPO). Service quality has dropped, every transaction costs money, time lines are slipping.

Mantri is another Bangalore-based builder. In the late 1990s, Mantri made a humble start by building economical houses for the middle class in the Bangalore suburb of Bannerghata. They delivered on commitments, were one of the few builders open to customization, and their service was exceptional. Mantri has slowly grown in stature and today boasts multiple high-end projects all across Bangalore. Mantri is a classic example of a company that has built trust and credibility by delivering on commitments.

Bose is renowned the world over for making quality speakers and sound systems. The CEO of Bose is once said to have commented 'I will never take my company public and get listed because that will kill innovation in my company.'

ICICI Bank is another classic example of a successful company that is straining itself at its edge. In terms of growth, the bank has few parallels in India, but the quality of service has deteriorated over the years. I have been banking with ICICI Bank since 1995. Over the years, the experience has been wonderful, I have had relationship managers who have given sound advise and there have been no hassles in working with them. My last relationship manager was Manisha Agnihotri. The level of trust and faith I bestowed on her was enormous. To me ICICI Bank was Manisha and she surpassed my expectations on all counts. One fine day Manisha decided to leave ICICI and all hell broke lose. The new incumbent called me after two months asking for my portfolio since the bank had no copy of the same. It took us three months of escalation and meetings to finally build the portfolio. Once that was done, I was clear that while the bank had grown, its systems were suspect. Since then I have decided to end my 10 year relationship with ICICI Bank and move on.

Many Indian businesses, including the BPO companies, need to ask themselves whether they want growth or healthy growth. And healthy growth is not measured purely by revenue, earning per share (EPS) and EBIDTA growth.

Take the case of Reliance—what started from Vimal and textiles has spread to refineries, telecom, retail, energy, special economic zones (SEZs), the list goes on. Here is a company that runs a business and ploughs the money back. Today it is growing like a hydra-headed monster. The Ambani brothers are already the richest in the world and the game has just begun.

The wealth that has been created by Indian IT/BPO companies through valuations that have been sky high is phenomenal—we are talking billions of dollars here. What is spent on innovation is a pittance. Where is this wealth? It is invested in mutual funds and earns tax-free dividends for share-holders. What a waste of money. This same amount can be used to develop human capital and to promote innovation.

There was a time when sales heads, CEOs, and controllers were the managers who used to look at each deal and question its long-term viability. Compliance and finance teams used to act independent of the CEO to create a balanced situation. Today, the industry is transforming. People responsible for scrutinizing and ensuring compliance are the ones pushing things to closure without calculating the impact. The need for a healthy pipeline and order book to drive the valuations is making the industry look at a very short-term picture.

Good dedicated managers and leaders who think long term are rare to come by and the lure of the stock market makes it even worse. This is a fundamental area of rethink for corporations not just in the BPO space but even in the IT market.

The Role of a Manager

Who is a good manager? What is his responsibility toward his team? Is he a mentor and a coach, or a driver? These are fundamental questions we need to ask.

When we started our careers in the early 1990s, the manager was a friend, philosopher, and guide. Managers took pride in developing and grooming their team members. You learnt from your manager, you looked up to him, you respected him, and you quietly took a dressing down from him. A good manager used to groom a successor and move on to a higher role.

Things have changed drastically today. Many managers today look at their direct reportees as potential threats. Across corporations you will find large gaps between heads of functions, line managers, and their direct reportees. This stems from two things—mediocrity and insecurity. A mediocre manager will never hire a person who is more qualified than him. He also knows that if he is over 40 years of age, jobs outside the company are not easy to come by. He tries every trick in the book to hang on to his role, which, in many cases, means being a yes man to his boss.

In the early years, you started as an individual contributor and after five–six years took on the responsibility of leading a team. Every year a few more people got added. It was a step-by-step learning. There is no MBA programme for being a manager. You need to learn it through the mistakes you make every day.

193

In a BPO environment, you have 23-year-olds managing teams of 10–15 people. They are just not geared for this. Both from the perspective of knowledge and maturity, 23-year-olds cannot handle 12–15 people who are in the same age group. The responsibility thrust on them is just too large. The team members do not look up to these young managers. When they cannot command respect, they start demanding it. That is the challenge in BPO companies where most people leave because of the manner in which they are treated by their managers.

Let us look at the life of an associate in a BPO firm. He has multiple bosses—his team leader (TL), the subject matter expert (SME) who is supposed to help him, the voice coach, the trainer, floor walkers, the command centre team. All of them are there to issue dictates and impose control systems. But who among them is concerned about the growth and development of the individual?

This is a problem across the corporation. The definition of a manager and his role has indeed changed drastically over the years.

Designations and Hierarchy

Let us compare a manufacturing unit with a BPO unit. A supervisor who manages a team in a manufacturing unit has at least five–six years of experience. He knows his job thoroughly and after having become an expert is now able to manage a team by guiding them and helping them. He takes another four–five years to move to the next level. There are many established manufacturing units where people become managers after 15 years of service. Even in IT companies, you need to be a coder for at least four–five years before you handle a team.

The high rate of attrition and burn out is forcing companies to show people a career path to reduce attrition. This is resulting in adding too many layers at the junior level with no clear job role augmentation. In many BPO companies you have the choice of becoming a TL, voice coach, trainer, level 2 specialist, etc., after having spent less than 12 months on the job as an agent. This trend continues and you see assistant vice presidents (AVPs) and general managers (GMs) with seven–eight years of work experience.

In any industry across the globe, when you think of a GM, you think of a seasoned professional, who has gone through three–four varied job roles and demonstrated business acumen. Not only is he adept at managing people, but has good interpersonal skills, has some domain expertise, and has strategic thinking abilities. In Japan, the US, and the Middle East, the GM designation is the senior-most designation, next only to that of the chief executive officer (CEO) and the chief managing director (CMD). It is higher than a vice president or a director. If you land at Dubai airport and your visiting card has a GM designation, you get priority treatment.

This definition sadly does not hold true in BPO companies. Designations are used as retention tools. Most people in senior management in the BPO industry would have been in the same role, worked with the same managers, been in one location and grown. They get promoted on the basis of the number of people reporting into them.

Indians by nature are designation conscious—if you give an employee a choice between a 20 per cent hike and a 10 per cent hike with a fancy designation, most people would opt for the latter.

The difference between India and the US is the lack of correlation between designations and job role. Individual contributors in the US can never be managers. In India, you will find many individual contributors who are GMs. The mistake being made in the Indian industry is the linkage of salary with designations. In the US, you can have a specialist programme manager with 20 years of experience earning a salary of US$ 200,000, which may higher than that of his manager. This would never happen in Indian BPO companies.

Can a GM or a VP from the BPO industry move to the IT world with the same designation? It is doubtful. But can a senior manager from the hotel industry or airlines industry move in as a GM in the BPO industry? That is highly probable! That kind of sums up the situation in the BPO industry today.

The definition of R&R (rewards and recognition) has changed to resign and re-negotiate across BPO companies. If one person uses this tactic successfully, it soon becomes a trend across the company and is used unabashedly even by the top management.

Designations are supposed to reward performance, identify stature and role, and motivate people. This is not happening in most BPO companies. Most companies also do not have a well defined transparent policy for promotions at senior levels. This trend is disturbing. It sets up wrong expectations and causes dissatisfaction amongst many older employees.

Industry and human resources (HR) managers need to ponder on such tactical moves and on whether they augur well for the industry in the long run.

Building Brands—How to Differentiate Yourself

Between 1995 and 2007, the Indian economy has been on the run—notching growth rates in excess of 8 per cent year after year. The spending power of people has increased and the 'dream' middle class is choking the malls to capacity.

During this unprecedented boom—let us look back and see how many brands have established themselves as innovative market leaders—delivering on scale and quality.

We asked over 20 people of different age groups—children, women, students and professionals at random about the top brands in India. The four names that were mentioned unanimously were Airtel, Café Coffee Day, Kingfisher Airlines and the Future Group (Big Bazaar, Pantaloon, etc.). They are there all over the place and growing at a scale and size that is unprecedented. They have excelled with both product and service. They have been innovative and stand out in the crowd. They have dreamt big and delivered on their dreams. India should be proud of these companies.

A decade back, nobody had heard these names and today they touch the lives of millions on a daily basis. In a country where the big get bigger and most new initiatives are started by the Tatas, Ambanis, Birlas, and Mahindras, it is impressive to note that barring Kingfisher all the other brands have been created by first-generation entrepreneurs.

A company like Airtel, which has millions of customers across the country, delivers on service. I recently called up the Airtel call centre to fix a problem on my broadband connection. I called at 3.30 p.m. on a Friday evening. I promptly got through and was told the following, 'Sir we will solve your problem by 9.30 tomorrow, else we will give you a credit of Rs 500'. I was pleasantly surprised as this was least expected. It was a first time experience for me. I did not have to wait till the next day. The problem was solved by 5.30 p.m. the same day.

Why do we have only four such successful brands and not 20? Why do we not as a country have an equivalent of McDonalds? Why could Nirulas not grow beyond north India? Why did Thumbs Up sell off to Coke even before the war had begun? Why is Saravana Bhavan even after 20 years a successful brand only in Chennai? (They have had success in New Delhi and have expanded to foreign shores, but what stops them from becoming a 1,000-joint establishment in India, opening a branch every week?) Why does MTR have only two outlets in Bangalore? Why does Haldiram have less than 10 establishments when it is a much loved and successful brand? The list of successful brands and companies that are happy at having tasted success, but have no desire to scale and grow at the speed of most global brands, can go on and on.

We see this trend even amongst Indian BPO companies. The initial start-ups wanted to sell and make a quick buck. Spectramind, Daksh, and Customer Asset are all examples of companies started by successful entrepreneurs, who decided to sell off their companies when they realized that it would be a challenge to manage large-scale operations.

While the country has no dearth of entrepreneurs, most of them lack the staying power and the ability to run a marathon.

The growth of the BPO industry has opened up avenues in sourcing, training, background checks, and transportation. The opportunity is large—the sourcing market for IT/BPO is alone close to Rs 11 billion. The market is again fragmented with the largest players in the Rs 500–600 million range and thousands in the Rs 10–100 million range.

The core value for Brand India in IT/BPO is low cost. That is a good entry strategy. But if you are the largest in the world, that strategy has to change. Our realization per associate and rate per hour in the BPO industry at US$ 10–18 is clearly the lowest in the world, while our desire for profits are the highest. It is inevitable that we choke the system to try and squeeze out every drop of efficiency.

Marketing as a profession and brand building in IT/BPO companies is limited. Budgets are sparse—it is less than 1 per cent of the revenue and is spent mainly on customer events and collaterals. Marketing investment is seen as adding more sales people.

In a fast moving consumer goods (FMCG) company, marketing is the first priority for the CEO. The industry attracts some of the smartest brains from business schools. The best of marketing talent tends to stay away from IT/BPO companies. Their role here is limited. Budgets tend to yo-yo based on quarterly profits and the work is mundane—building websites, creating collaterals, a few audio-visuals, and, in some cases, corporate communications.

The thrust to create a marketing team that covers the customer, employee, and the eco-system is lacking. A company that can put this together and attract the right talent to drive this will stand out and in the long run benefit by building a sustained brand value proposition.

Branding need not always be done by the central marketing team. Applied marketing is the need of the day. Packaging content and creating crisp communication to employees and to prospective hires during induction can have a positive impact.

When I took over the people supply chain function in Wipro BPO, we clearly saw the need to apply marketing in everything that we did. We analysed the information need and touch points at every level from the time a person walks in for an interview till he completes the induction process. We then looked at areas where the same information was being asked a number of times. We looked at the different photocopied forms that were being distributed at different stages of the selection process. After analysing all this we consolidated all the information in a comprehensive joining kit. We saved cost and time while making a lasting impression. Hundreds of candidates came back and said that this was the first time that they had seen something like this.

We went on to change the manner in which the offer letter was worded. We made it simple and answered some frequently asked questions in it. The result was that fewer clarifications were sought in the first 30 days. The new recruits were not in for any unpleasant surprise when they received their first pay cheque.

Marketing can be applied in everything you do. HR, finance, operations—every manager has to be conscious and apply thought on improving things around him. How do you package the CEO award, how do you customize the trophy, how should the mailer be designed so that it stands out—there is so much that can be done at every level to make an impact.

Brands are built because they make a lasting impression—the finishing touch is crucial.

Nilgiris is a leading retail chain in Bangalore and Chennai. It was started in 1905 and had a few stores. Nilgiris recently opened two new outlets in Koramangla, a Bangalore suburb where I stay. The shop was on a prominent main road, the exterior of the shop was very well done—it was bright and looked inviting. We decided to walk in and do our monthly shopping. The shop was well stocked, the aisles were well managed, help was available to locate things, and we found the experience enjoyable. The shop was brimming with people and it was actually difficult to manoeuvre the fully laden trolleys we had.

We landed at the payment counter—there were three of them, but only two were staffed (at peak time, at the beginning of the month). It took us 20 minutes to reach the counter (we had spent 20 minutes shopping) and were finally face-to-face with a hassled looking girl who looked less than 18 years old, who was doing the billing. The scanner she was using was not effective; she tried scanning the items twice or thrice before typing in the bar code manually. I was surprised to see that more than 50 per cent of the items could not be scanned. And this is what was causing the delay.

This is a good example of the finishing touch. You set up a nice shop in a prominent place, pay hefty rents, get the crowd in, impress them with your stock and price, and finally cut corners on the scanners you buy. It spoils the entire experience of shopping. I had a similar experience at Reliance Retail and have decided not to go there for some time.

Two critical touch points in retail are the trolley you use and the experience at the payment counter. If you fail here, the entire brand experience comes down.

Why do we cut corners in the last leg? Restaurants are often stingy with tissue paper and hesitate to give customers more than one. Even McDonalds in India has become stingy on the number of ketchup packs they give you.

Jet airways revolutionized airline services in India when they started; Kingfisher bettered it. Indian Airlines, Jet Airways, and Kingfisher all use airlines from Boeing or Airbus, but it is the service of their ground staff, their crew, the way they package and serve the food that distinguishes one airline from the other. Jet is the fastest to load luggage on to the baggage conveyor after its flight has landed. As a priority customer you feel thrilled to be walking out with your luggage just minutes after landing. With good quality service, most business travellers would not hesitate to pay a premium for Jet or Kingfisher over Indian Airlines.

If you differentiate and deliver superior service, you can demand a premium. If you need to build brands you cannot be penny wise, pound foolish.

Why can BPO companies not do the same? If their quality of service is superior, why can their brand not fetch them rates that are 40–50 per cent higher than the current rates (which would still be significantly cheaper than global rates)? Thinking in this direction will set the wheels in motion for the total transformation of the industry.

During campus recruitment, a job in Hindustan Lever or Proctor and Gamble would be a dream for someone interested in marketing, for a finance professional it would be a job with Citibank, for someone interested in consultancy it would be a job with Mckenzie or Accenture. What would be the dream job for a person keen to join a BPO? Many colleges in New Delhi and Mumbai have started denying BPO companies permission to come for campus interviews. One option for BPOs is to quietly slink away to campuses in second and third-tier cities.

What are BPO companies doing to sell themselves as dream destinations. BPOs are probably the only companies that can offer you 50 different roles during a 10-year career. It pays well and gives employees rapid growth and learning. And yet it is not marketed as a dream job.

Outsourcing from a BPO

BPO stands for business process outsourcing. Do companies that sell the mantra of outsourcing practice what they preach?

For every employee who works in a BPO, there are four other jobs generated. Definitely there is a lot of outsourcing that happens—transport, catering services, and administrative services are outsourced. But these are services that have traditionally been outsourced.

The core of a BPO is delivering value to customers by doing work in an efficient manner. Calls need to be handled and transactions carried out in the stipulated time frame. Employees need to be taken care of well.

There are a host of ancillary services that can be outsourced. The trend has started and we expect this to accelerate in the coming months and years. With the pressure on profitability, companies will look at cutting costs and the number of people involved in ancillary activities.

Many companies have started looking around for help, but are yet to see capable partners who can deliver. Many of the ancillary services are run by mom and pop shops that are happy with the one or two customers they have. Indian industry is yet to see many graduates from the Indian Institute of Technology (IIT) and Indian Institute of Management (IIM) starting a transport business or a cafeteria business or even a recruitment consultancy.

The Indian mindset values a job in a multinational corporation (MNC) or an Indian corporate house much more than a self-owned business. Highly educated individuals do join their family business, but starting off something on one's own is a trend that is just beginning.

This throws up great opportunities for people who have confidence in their abilities. The risk factor is not large. If the market is large and growing, all you need to do is deliver and do a good job to grab a piece of the pie.

Payroll outsourcing, recruitment process outsourcing, employee branding, training, counselling, and even marketing are areas that can get outsourced. Not only will they deliver cost benefits to companies, but will also help companies in their core business in the future.

The transaction piece can get outsourced—companies need to focus on the transformation piece, says Aashu Kalappa, head of HR at First Source.

The most important thing in outsourcing work is to have a robust process. Never outsource something that is not working within your own organization. If you cannot fix the problem, your vendor cannot either. Once you have achieved stability with an activity and the process is documented and proven, then you are ready to go.

While companies have not looked at second-level outsourcing, it is something that is bound to happen soon. Large companies as super vendors will have the muscle power to pick up large contracts. They have the money power to afford a sales force in the US and Europe. Entry-level work like data entry, finance and accounts, email, and chat will get outsourced to smaller players. Yes, it will reduce an organization's margin, but it will give them time and energy to focus on the high value addition work that gets them the top dollars.

Employee Branding

Ask a BPO employee in Wipro or EDS or Infosys who they work for and the answer will be Hewlett-Packard (HP) or Dell or AOL (America Online) or Microsoft. Most employees correlate with the process they work for—they just walk into an office with the company's brand name. As they keep switching jobs, the confusion gets even bigger. How do you build a brand and inculcate a value system in employees in this scenario?

The differentiation, if any, can come only from the touch points in day-to-day activities. Right from the time a person joins an organization, the experiences he has is what makes him value the brand. How was the engagement between the offer of a job and joining? Did the first month's pay come on time? Did all queries get answered on time? Is the help desk manned by people who can answer queries? How easy is it to navigate the company's official question and answer site? Commit and deliver is the keystone to building a strong employee brand. Transparency in policies is the icing on the cake. This sounds simple, but most companies struggle to deliver on these.

Across levels, people want to look at role models who can inspire them. Role models are flag-bearers of a company's ideology and its values. They are mentors and guides who can help people in their journey.

Most companies confuse employee branding with fun and parties. In a high pressure work environment fun is a necessity but that is just one small element of employee branding.

Employee branding is an area that touches all interactions you have in a company. It is not the responsibility of HR alone. It is an area that requires an eye for detail, a high sense of empathy and the finishing touch. It is time companies had a dedicated department for employee branding that could work through all the functions to achieve this.

BPO and Six Sigma

Non-linear growth, value-added service, higher productivity through tools and automation, optimization, enhanced efficiency, standardization and simplification—these are some of the key strategic drivers we see across companies in the BPO industry. All this is an effort to move from a cost arbitrage platform to a value proposition model. These will help improve customer engagement and help retain them while enabling growth with higher profits. In a nutshell, it is an attempt to be different.

To achieve this, companies are trying to use the time-tested and accepted methodology of Six Sigma for improving the efficiency and effectiveness of their operations.

Most BPOs have been hiring Six Sigma black belts and process consultants. There is no doubt on the effectiveness of Six Sigma, but there is not much thought on how Six Sigma needs to be implemented for a BPO. Can the manufacturing or IT model work in a BPO or is there a need for customization? These are questions which we need to answer.

Any Six Sigma project would ideally take 8–12 weeks to complete. Given the dynamic nature of the BPO business, many of the assumptions that we start with change during this period.

Six Sigma can definitely be used in areas like attrition control and transport effectiveness, but you cannot run a Six Sigma project to determine why the customer satisfaction (CSAT) scores dipped or why revenue is dropping. Implementing LEAN would be a better way of solving these problems.

LEAN owes its origin to the manufacturing industry and involves incremental improvements based on feedback from people working on the project as they are best suited to suggest improvements. It is a powerful concept that has been used with immense benefits in the automobile industry. Six Sigma focuses on defect removal and LEAN focuses on enhancements and improvements at each step.

Quality teams across BPOs need to understand the LEAN model better than Six Sigma concepts to be able to deliver value.

Are We Doing Enough? Corporate Social Responsibility

In an earlier section we had talked about workplace stress and its impact in the BPO industry. This area has till now been largely ignored by the industry.

While the external factors are difficult to change, the employer- and employee-controlled factors can be addressed suitably to reduce stress. Counselling, proactive measures, and being a listening organization can go a long way in reducing workplace stress.

Recently, the health minister of India suggested improvements in BPOs to help ease the stress and tension of employees. Night shifts, long hours, bad posture, all lead to severe health problems amongst the youth. The response from the industry and leading bodies like the National Association of Software and Services Companies (NASSCOM) was defensive. This was one rare occasion where a minister had touched upon a point that was relevant to employees; the industry's reaction was surprising.

Having to adhere to a certain level of government stipulated rules and regulations may help the industry bring in standardization, which would be in the long-term interest of BPO employees.

The BPO industry in the Philippines has to follow strict government regulations about the number of hours of work, the mandatory payment of the 13th month's salary on a pro rata basis at the time of resignation, etc. Such government initiatives have helped the industry and the employees.

The Indian industry needs to be open to such ideas and look at the positives before vehemently opposing them. If the industry has to grow from a strength of 600,000 employees to a few million in the years to come, best practices from across the globe need to be looked at to make the Indian BPO industry a better place.

The other area in which the industry can play a significant role is in working closely with education institutions to increase the number of people joining the industry. Less than 15 per cent of engineers and graduates passing from India's colleges and universities are employable. Companies need to adopt colleges in small towns and work closely with the staff to develop courses that will allow them to be absorbed in productive jobs at the time of graduation. Here again it is a mindset of investing for the long term. Manufacturing companies set up plants with a long-term vision. Similarly, BPO companies need to look at near hire programmes that will increase the conversion percentage in phases from 15 to 25 to 50 per cent. A lot of investment and grass-roots development work is needed in this area.

The BPO industry is today in its adolescent phase. The future direction it takes will depend on how the people running the business manoeuvre it from here on. Just as an adolescent needs independence and hand holding to flourish, so does the BPO industry.

In conclusion, the key points to remember are:

1. Focus on value growth as opposed to volume growth.
2. Look at optimization and key differentiators as opposed to cost and labour arbitrage.
3. Invest for the future.
4. Build a strong BPO brand that attracts people and acts as an engine of growth in second and third-tier cities.
5. Lastly, remember that this is a people business and not a commodity business.

It takes effort from the employees, employers and the eco-system to achieve this goal.

Glossary of Industry Terms

Business Functions/Processes

BAM	business activity monitoring
BE	business efficiency/business excellence
BFS	banking, finance, and securities
BPO	business processes outsourcing
BS 7799	IT and information security standard
BU	business unit
CAG	customer advocacy group
CCOD	call centre operations desk
CMIS	central management information system
COBC	code of business conduct
comp offs	compensatory time off, earned by an employee for time spent in office during a non-working day
COPC	customer-oriented process certification
CWFM	central workforce management
CTC	cost to company
E-learning	Education/training through online web-based courses
EFF	electronic foot fall
F&A	finance and accounting

HR	human resources
IS	information security
ISO	International Organization for Standardization (Organisation Internationale de Normalisation), widely known as ISO, is an international standard-setting body composed of representatives from various national standards organizations
KA	knowledge acquisition
KPA	key performance areas
KPI	key performance indicators (these are financial and non-financial metrics used to quantify objectives to reflect strategic performance of an organization)
KPM	key performance metrics
KPO	knowledge processes outsourcing
MBR	monthly business review
MIS	management information systems (it is a general name for the academic discipline covering the application of people, technologies, and procedures—collectively called information systems—to solve business problems)
MSA	master services agreement
OJT	on the job training
OPS	operations
OT	overtime
PMS	payroll management system/ performance management system
POA	plan of action
QBR	quarterly business review

QMS	quality management system
R&R	rewards and recognition
Roster	list of people by which to regulate their duties
SBU	strategic business unit
SCM	supply chain management
SEP	skill enhancement programme
SLA	service level agreement (SLA is that part of a service contract where the level of service is formally defined)
SOW	statement of work (SOW is a document used in the systems development life cycle. An organization desiring to have some work done, that is, the prospective customer, produces a SOW as part of a request for proposals.)
Sox	Sarbanes-Oxley Act of 2002 (a United States federal securities law, sometimes also called SOx)
SS	strategic sourcing (recruitment)
TP	transaction processing
TQ	transition queue
TT	talent transformation
Voice and accent	communication tool kit
week offs	offs earned in a week

Metrics Related and Miscellaneous Terms

ACW	after call work
AHT	averaging handling time (it is the sum of average talk time, average hold time and average ACW)

ANI	automated number identification (the calling number display for the call receiver)
ARR	agent resolve rate (problem-solving rate of an agent)
ASA	Average speed of answer (a measurement expressing the time taken for a call to be answered either by an agent or auto attendant)
ATT	Average talk time
AUX	auxiliary mode (breaks)
bench	any resources that are non-productive for their role (non-occupied resources)
bulge	ratio of non-productive resources to productive resources from a process level at every hierarchy level
call flow	incoming calls traffic
call release	disconnection of the call received by the agent on the floor
cold calling	telemarketing to prospects with whom there is no established relationship
CPM	critical performance metrics
CSAT	customer satisfaction
dual line	the line that allows inbound calling and outbound calling
fatal error	an error that is not acceptable and if committed the quality score becomes '0'
FTF	first time fix rate (a rate of resolving customer issues/queries at the first customer contact instance)
FTR	first time resolve rate (rate of resolving customer issues/queries)

HT/hold	hold time
inbound	the calls received by the customer
intelligent routing	the routing of calls through predefined business rules that are based upon the expected characteristics of the caller
involuntary attrition	when the organization decides the employee should leave
IVR	interactive voice response (a system that interacts with callers using predetermined menus and telephone key input, or speech recognition software)
outbound	calls made to the customer
PABX	private automatic branch exchange (the switch, which manages calls within an organization)
queue time	operating timelines for a sub process of an account
scorecard	a group of performance indicators that reflect the operations of the centre
shrinkage	an allocation of time from rosters that accounts for unscheduled breaks, that is, unplanned leave
SL	service level
SOP	standard operating principles
stack ranking	stack ranking is the relative ranking of employees in a department, organization, etc., which is indicative of their performance
throughput	ratio of output to input
toll free	free of cost
voice response	use of a pre-recorded message to answer incoming calls

| VOIP | voice over internet protocol (a system that enables voice calls to be carried over a data network) |
| XPR | external problem resolution |

People/Roles

agents	employee servicing customers on phone also known as associates, customer service agents or FTEs
billable FTE	billable full-time equivalent
CCP	customer care professional
CEO	chief executive officer
CFO	chief finance officer
COO	chief operating officer
CSR	customer service representative
EM	escalation manager
FTE	full-time equivalent
GL	group leader
HOD	head of department
L1	level 1 technician
L2	level 2 technician
L3	level 3 technician
non-billable FTE	full-time equivalent who has not started to generate revenue(for example, agents in training)
ops manager	operations manager
PRC	process risk champion
PRO	process relationship officer
process owner	head of a business account/process
QA	quality analyst
QAP	quality audit personnel

RS	resolution specialist
SDL	service delivery leader
SGL	senior group leader
SME	subject matter expert
SPOC	single point of contact
TL	team leader
TM	team manager
voice coach	coaches on shop floor dedicated for FTEs communication skills

Time Related

CMS supervisor	call servicing tool
COB	close of business
comp offs	compensatory holidays taken by FTE and employees working on floor in lieu of holidays declared by state/central government
EOD	end of day
FW	fiscal week
FY	fiscal year
graveyard shift	shift from 11:30 p.m. to 4 a.m.
MTD	month to date
NBD	next business day
QTD	quarter to date
roster	time allocation table for all agents
shift	working hours for employees
week offs	mandatory offs in a week given to all employees not necessarily Saturday and Sunday
YTD	year to date

Work Processes

access card	an electronic card programmed to allow access to specific areas/premises in the organization
action items	measures to be taken or activities to be conducted against pending issues or corrective feedback
bandwidth	available resources
BGV	background verification check
calibration	standardizing scoring of assessment or methodology of evaluation
CRM	customer relationship management (a process that records customer contacts and information to allow for an enhanced relation with the customer)
DTS	disciplinary track sheet
employee referral	candidates referred by employee of an organization
induction	acquainting candidates with the organization, its business, and structure

About the Authors

V. Anandkumar (VAK) and Subhasish Biswas are mechanical engineers from the 1992 batch. VAK graduated from the Regional Engineering College, Surat and Subhasish from the Indian Institute of Technology, Kharagpur. Subhasish then went on to complete his masters of business administration from the Indian Institute of Management, Ahmedabad.

VAK is a creative change agent who has worked in the information technology (IT)/business process outsourcing (BPO)/telecommunications sectors in India and the United States (US) in diverse areas spanning sales, marketing, programme management, and human resources (HR). He has been one of the early proponents of employee branding and has rolled out mass employee connect programmes. Subhasish is a Six Sigma black belt with vast experience in execution and project management in the construction, engineering, and BPO industries. His core expertise is in delivery and applying quality tools to enhance productivity.

Both VAK and Subhasish have been drivers of change across their careers. They have high levels of empathy and are passionate about nurturing human capital and helping employees scale greater heights, an area of focus in the BPO industry. In this volume, VAK's marketing skill and expertise in the field of HR blend with Subhasish's analytical skills to create a product that is potent and on target.

Having been associated closely with the BPO industry and seen its growth and enormous potential, the authors have, through this book, made an attempt to fix the foundation to ensure that the sublime edifice of the BPO industry can continue to grow stronger and taller over the years.